THE ACCIDENTAL PALEO

**EASY VEGETARIAN RECIPES
FOR A PALEO LIFESTYLE**

LAUREN LOBLEY

The Accidental Paleo: Easy Vegetarian Recipes for a Paleo Lifestyle
Copyright © 2018 Lauren Lobley. All rights reserved.

ISBN: 978-1-939563-45-3

Library of Congress Cataloging in Publication Control Number: 2017053644

Editor: Tracy Kearns
Cover Design: Janée Meadows and Caroline De Vita
Interior Design and Layout: Caroline De Vita
Photos: Aprilia Love
Copyediting, Proofreading, and Indexing: Tim Tate

Primal Blueprint Publishing, 1641 S. Rose Ave., Oxnard, CA 93033
Please contact the publisher with any questions, concerns, and feedback, or to obtain quantity discounts.
888-774-6259 or 310-317-4414
email: info@primalblueprintpublishing.com, or visit PrimalBlueprintPublishing.com.

DISCLAIMER: The ideas, concepts, and opinions expressed in this book are intended to be used for educational purposes only. This book is sold with the understanding that the author and publisher are not rendering medical advice of any kind, nor is this book intended to replace medical advice, nor to diagnose, prescribe, or treat any disease, condition, illness, or injury. It is imperative that before beginning any diet, exercise, recipes, or lifestyle program, including any aspect of the methodologies mentioned in *The Accidental Paleo,* you receive full medical clearance from a licensed physician. If you are currently taking medication for health conditions, are pregnant or a growing youth, or have a current or past condition such as cardiovascular disease, cancer, diabetes, or other serious health conditions, major dietary changes should be considered with extreme caution and the guidance of a trusted medical professional. The author and publisher claim no responsibility to any person or entity for any liability, loss, or damage caused or alleged to be caused directly or indirectly as a result of the use, application, or interpretation of the material in this book. If you object to this disclaimer, you may return the book to publisher for a full refund.

For Cassandra, who helped me discover my inner chef.

*For my lulus, who opened me up in ways I will never
be able to truly thank you for.*

*And for my family—especially Mom, Dad, Jarrett, Jillian,
Auntie Lissa, my husband Ted, my daughter Madison
Grace, and my family-friends, the ones who aren't blood
related but who feel like family just the same.*

*Thank you for loving me through every step of this
journey—and helping me get here in the first place.*

Table of Contents

THE ACCIDENTAL PALEO

Foreword

by Anthony "Tony" Horton

I've been very fortunate to find success and happiness in helping others to fulfill their health and fitness goals. From P90X to Double Time, people are not only changing physically, but mentally and emotionally, too. Their relationships, energy, memory, sleep, and enthusiasm for life is better as well. When people approach me to express how one of my programs has changed their life, it never ceases to amaze me. I had hoped to grow up doing something that would help people, but this life has been better than anything I could have ever imagined.

In my 30 years as a trainer I've learned along the way that THE critical piece to getting fit and healthy starts with food and nutrition. I've experimented with various "diets" throughout my adult life (which was a departure from my Standard American Diet (SAD) as a kid), and I'm still exploring new ways of fueling my body and mind to maximize the quality of my life. One thing I know for sure is that "clean eating" is at the core of any rock-solid health and exercise plan, no matter how you slice it.

For the past decade I've been amazed at Lauren's ability to create recipes to satisfy both my carnivorous and plant-based eating habits, and I'm always blown away by how much incredible flavor and texture she manages to get into everything she prepares.

This cookbook is a supreme sampling of her work. I know you'll find the recipes as delicious as I have throughout the years. Lauren's dedication to wellness and her craft—food—was evident from the moment I met her, and I know her passion shines through on every page.

Her philosophy to health and nutrition is refreshing. It's approachable. It's flexible, and it's easy. So, if you've been looking for new ways to get some vegan/vegetarian paleo recipes into your life, you've picked the right book.

Every meal is an opportunity to make a healthier choice.

So, eat the best, and forget the rest.
Tony Horton

Tony Horton is the wildly popular creator of the best-selling fitness series: P90X®, P90X2®, P90X3®, and Ten Minute Trainer®, and most recently his 22-Minute military inspired workout, 22 Minute Hard Corps®. Tony is a **world-class motivational speaker** and the **author** of top-selling books *Bring It!*, *Crush It!*, and *The Big Picture: 11 Laws That Will Change Your Life*. He has appeared on countless television programs as a **fitness and lifestyle expert** to promote healthy living through exercise and proper nutrition.

http://www.tonyhortonlife.com/

Introduction

I am a mostly plant-based, sometimes fish-eating, off-and-on egg-loving, gluten/dairy/sugar-free foodie with a passion for making healthy food taste good. In theory, I'm essentially a vegetarian. But I'm also paleo. As a recovering sugar addict and former pastry chef, no one could be more surprised by this turn of events in my diet than me.

I didn't always eat this way.

I am the daughter of a full-blooded Italian mama and an Irish/British papa. Dad didn't have much of a palate for anything but meat and potatoes, but my mom? Pasta sauce ran through her veins. Admittedly, she didn't enjoy cooking (sorry, Mom, but you know it's true), but she always managed to feed us some pretty amazing meals. Dad's job was on the BBQ, where he burnt many a steak, pork chop, and potato and then lovingly served it up to us, claiming that the burnt part was where the flavor is. We begged to differ.

My grandmother was your stereotypical Italian grandma: always with an apron tied around her waist, a wooden spoon in her hand, and a pot of pasta and meatballs on the stove. We used to drive late at night from Montreal to Toronto—a five-and-a-half-hour journey (and yes, I'm Canadian) to her house. Inevitably, when we arrived, whether at some ungodly hour of the night or early morning, she would fill our bowls with steaming hot pasta, meatballs, and sauce. No matter the time, food was always the main attraction.

You would think that having grown up with such a grandmother that I would have had an affinity for cooking at a young age. Yet, this couldn't be further from the truth. My immature palate much preferred the SAD (Standard American Diet): delicious chocolate cake, hot dogs with ketchup on a white bun, every brand of cookie down the cookie aisle, pizza with cheese, pasta with butter, bread with gobs of more butter, and lots and lots of soda (or as we call it in Canada, pop). I'm sure that trying to get me to eat anything green gave my mother premature wrinkles and grey hair. The closest she could get was iceberg lettuce, but only if it was smothered in bottled ranch or Italian dressing. And even then, I would plug my nose and force it down.

In fact, it wasn't until my mid-20s that I began to regularly eat green vegetables, eventually, swapping out meat, dairy, and even gluten for, well, more vegetables, grains I had never heard of (quinoa), and even more veggies.

I wouldn't make the shift to a mostly plant-based, gluten-free diet until 2010 (and I wouldn't realize it was actually more like a *paleo* vegetarian diet until 2016), but my journey toward a healthier diet ultimately began after a visit to LA in 2006. I was managing a lululemon store in Montreal, and I wasn't the best at it, to put it lightly. I had no idea how to manage people. I figured if you're the boss, people had to listen to you. Turns out, that's not how to create a harmonious work environment that everyone looks forward to working in.

Food changed all of that for me.

My boyfriend at the time and I visited friends in West Hollywood for vacation that year. My friend, Cassandra, had the Food Network on all day. I had never heard of the Food Network. Until then, my TV was reserved for *So You Think You Can Dance* and *Grey's Anatomy*. I was struck by how quickly and effortlessly Cassandra could put a charcuterie board together for all of us to nosh on while she prepared dinner. She even baked a cake from scratch!

"You know you can just get a boxed cake from the grocery store, right?" I told her smugly. Only now do I realize how incredibly silly that sounded, and in fact, as I type this, I wonder how she ever wanted to be my friend after that!

I was so flabbergasted that anyone would bake from scratch that I actually went to the store and purchased a Betty Crocker cake mix for her, baked it, and had her try it. She took a bite and agreed that it was okay (clearly, she was just being polite). Then we left and went for a walk, and when we got back, her dog Touque (French for "hat") had eaten the entire pan! I should have taken that as a sign of what was to come.

During that trip to La-La Land, I was mesmerized by the farmers' markets, the outdoor living, the cooking channel, and the ease with which Cassandra prepared food—food that I normally wouldn't eat, but that she prepared so amazingly I couldn't help but admit that I liked it. I even asked for seconds. It wasn't vegan, but it was paleo, healthy, and delicious.

This was my first experience with healthy food made from fresh ingredients that could not only taste good but that also was made with love.

So, when I got back to Montreal, I bought all of Ina Garten's cookbooks (seriously, all of them), along with my very first KitchenAid mixer (which I have to this day), and began experimenting. My boyfriend was a willing taste tester, yet it was too much food even for him to consume. So I began inviting my staff over for dinners. I figured if I could cook for them, they might start to see me as the goofy human that I was, and not as the type-A, "do-what-I-say" boss that I seemed to be projecting at work.

I was not prepared for what came next. The barriers between my staff and I slowly began to melt away as we dined together. Even more amazingly, I began to understand that being a manager is not about telling coworkers what to do, but rather, it's about becoming invested in them and deeply and truly caring about their wellbeing. I learned that as a leader, you don't manage people. You manage conversations, and in particular, the conversations going on inside people's heads. If you're a bad leader (read, a leader who doesn't pay attention to your coworkers' strengths, weakness, dreams, and goals), you can bet that the conversations people are having about you in their heads are not productive, and therefore, you're not going to help your people achieve their fullest potential (which is what you want in any business, in my opinion). Great leaders listen. They practice empathy. They encourage dialogue. I learned that at lululemon. By inviting my staff into my home and letting them see me for who I really was (a goofy gal who likes to cook) rather than the person I showed up as at work (a type-A boss with no wiggle room), I learned not only what great leaders look like, but also, how being a great leader can help others become great leaders, too.

After a few months, everything transformed. I stopped being so hard on myself, and not surprisingly, on my staff. I began to operate with compassion and to see that things are not always black and white. Creativity resides in everyone, and sometimes rules should be bent, if not broken. I am grateful for the opportunity to transform my way of working with others because it profoundly changed how I saw myself and my coworkers and it gave me the opportunity to become more connected.

And all of it is thanks to food.

The transformative power of food has inspired me ever since. When I moved to LA with lululemon in 2008, I began assistant-managing an entirely new set of people at a new store in a foreign country. I was nervous that they might be thinking, "Who is this chick who thinks she can just come in here and run things?"

So, I did what I now knew best: I cooked for them. I bought a green picnic table from the flea market on La Brea and Fairfax, and every other week I would host my staff at what became one of my infamous potlucks. It was truly amazing.

A few years later, I decided to cut the cord and go to culinary school. It was my dream to open up a bakery that could also double as a community center. Much like the lululemon model, I wanted to create a space for people to connect over food and experience its transformative powers the way I had a few years before.

Somewhere between 2008 and 2010, after watching a documentary called *Earthlings* and because of a lifetime's worth of digestive problems, I stopped eating meat completely. My culinary school journey began in September of 2010. I loved it. And I hated it. I was gaining weight. I was feeling lethargic. I was feeling foggy. All of the gluten and sugar I was consuming in my pastry classes was making me sick. I decided it was time to make a change: I cut out gluten and sugar. Low and behold, the inflammation in my body receded, my weight dropped down to a healthier one, and my mind cleared.

So, I shifted focus. Now, instead of opening a regular bakery, I would instead open a vegan and gluten-free one. I moved back to LA in 2011 to be with my now husband and got to work on the business plan. In the meantime, I was fortunate enough to secure a job as the head baker with renowned pastry chef and Food Network star Duff Goldman, where I remained employed for a year-and-a-half.

As I baked cakes (by the end, I was baking 2,700 cakes and too many thousands of cupcakes a week) and looked toward opening my bakery, I couldn't shake this feeling.

While I still wanted to open a bakery, I knew that as a business owner, I wouldn't feel comfortable letting any of the pastries out the door without my having sampled them first. And even though my concept was gluten free and vegan, it still contained one very powerful ingredient: sugar.

And that wasn't OK with me. I decided that as a healthy person (my husband and I own and operate a yoga studio in Malibu, and we are both into trail running, skiing, and everything health and fitness), I simply could no longer stand for sugar.

I prepare and eat according to a vegetarian paleo diet. I eat fish sometimes, and eggs weekly, but the majority of my diet is made up of vegetables, non-dairy milk, nut butters, nuts, seeds, and a limited amount of fruits and legumes. I probably eat more legumes than any hard-core paleo eater is comfortable with, but it seems to work for my system. And by my definition of a healthy diet, you must eat what makes you feel good.

So, I did some soul searching, worked for a healthcare start-up, and eventually went to the Institute for Integrative Nutrition in New York to become a certified Health Coach. Since then, I have prided myself on not only helping people feel healthier, but also on making healthy food taste amazing. As a sugar-addicted kid who spent the first 20-plus years of my life only wanting simple carbs, butter, and sugar, I figured my palate would be the most discerning of all and the right one for the job.

That's what I've been doing ever since. I've had a website since 2010 called Delectable You: Recipes for Food and for Life, where I post articles about all aspects of health, along with recipes and cooking videos. I have a YouTube cooking channel (since 2014), with over a hundred recipes and cooking videos. And I self-published a cookbook in 2015 called *14 Day Nutrition Reset*.

Today, I prepare and eat according to a vegetarian paleo diet. I eat fish sometimes and eggs weekly, but the majority of my diet is made up of vegetables, non-dairy milk, nut butters, nuts, seeds, and a limited amount of fruits and legumes. I probably eat more legumes than any hard-core paleo eater is comfortable with, but it seems to work for my system. And by my definition of a healthy diet, you must eat what makes you feel good.

The Accidental Paleo is a collection of 10 years of recipe testing gone right (I've left the flops on the cutting room floor where they belong), along with all of my heart and soul. Healthy food can taste amazing. I'm going to show you how.

Organizing Your Kitchen for Success

Ever since becoming a mostly plant-based vegetarian paleo, I have found that in order to make my life easier, I have had to make some adjustments in the way I shop for food. Specifically, there are some staple ingredients that, if I always have on hand, allow me to easily create a feast for my entire family without any fuss, or more importantly, without any wasted time. No one wants to have to run out to the grocery store at the end of a long work day to pick up missing ingredients for dinner, or worse, in the middle of cooking dinner itself!

In my case, I'm not just feeding my family, but I'm also recipe testing on a weekly basis. Simply put: I don't have time to mess around. A well-stocked pantry, fridge, and freezer is the only way I can get the job done without any stress. Whenever one of my staple items is almost out (or down to the last jar or bag), I immediately write it down on a grocery pad I keep on the fridge so that I can pick it up on my weekly grocery run (or else order it online—I love the internet for this!).

Bottom line? Planning ahead will make your job of feeding yourself and your family much easier.

Organizing your kitchen for success organizes yourself for success. Here are some of my recommendations. Some of them lean more toward a vegetarian rather than a paleo diet, so please do what works best for you. If you're not into legumes or grains or anything else you see on this list, skip them. For whatever reason, they seem to work for me.

All ingredients are either organic or locally sourced whenever possible.

PANTRY

Baking Flours, Starches, and Other Necessities

Bob's Red Mill Gluten Free AP Baking Flour

Bob's Red Mill Sweet Sorghum Flour

Bob's Red Mill Paleo Flour

Bob's Red Mill Flaxseed Meal

Bob's Red Mill Coconut Flour

Almond meal or flour

Potato starch

Cocoa powder

Unsweetened shredded coconut

Dates

Raisins

Gluten-free oats

Steel cut oats

Canned coconut milk

Baking soda

Baking powder

Vegan chocolate chips

Canned plain pumpkin puree

Nuts & Seeds

Hemp seeds

Chia seeds

Sunflower seeds (sprouted, if possible)

Pumpkin seeds (sprouted, if possible)

Almonds (raw, organic)

Cashews (raw)

Pecans (raw)

Macadamia nuts (unsalted)

Hazelnuts

Pine nuts

Savory Items

Roasted red peppers (jar)

Beans (garbanzo, black bean, great white northern, kidney, red lentils, etc.), dried and canned

Quinoa

Wild rice

Dried nori sheets

Seaweed snacks

Canned plum tomatoes

Canned diced tomatoes

Canned tomato sauce

Sundried tomatoes

Canned artichokes

Salsa

Paleo crackers and snacks

Smoothie Must-Haves

Goji berry powder

Moringa powder

Your favorite protein powder

Cacao nibs

Spirulina

Barley grass powder

Chaga mushroom powder

Sweeteners & Other Treats

Coconut sugar

Coconut nectar

Pure maple syrup

Raw honey

85% dark chocolate

Your favorite protein bars

Oils & Vinegars

Extra virgin olive oil (EVOO), high quality for everyday use

Balsamic vinegar (no caramel color, please)

Apple cider vinegar

Coconut oil

Spices

Sea salt

Pepper

Cinnamon

Turmeric

Oregano

Thyme

Cumin

Garam masala

Ginger (fresh and powdered)

Must-Have Fruits & Veggies

Sweet potatoes

Winter squash (when in season)

Avocados

Cherry tomatoes

Yellow onions

Red onions

Garlic

Bananas

Other

Your favorite herbal teas (ginger, licorice root, nettle leaf, rose hips, lemon balm, chamomile, mint, raspberry leaf—my favorite brand is Traditional Medicinals)

Fridge

Almond butter and other nut butters (homemade or store-bought)

Almond milk (or other non-dairy milks, always unsweetened)

Coconut yogurt (or other non-dairy yogurts)

Coconut water

Aloe juice

Mixed greens (for making salads: arugula, spring mix, spinach)

Kale (curly or dino)

Cucumber

Carrots

Celery

Broccoli

Cauliflower

Fresh parsley

Fresh cilantro

Fresh ginger

Fresh turmeric root

Dijon mustard

Hot sauce (my fave is Cholula)

Siracha (my second favorite)

A 14-ounce can of coconut milk (for making coconut whipped cream in a pinch)

Eggs

Coconut aminos

Gluten-free soy sauce (tamari)

Toasted sesame seed oil

Chickpea miso paste (or regular miso paste if you don't mind soy)

Pickles (makes for a great snack)

Freezer

Coconut meat

Ice

Frozen veggies for smoothies (broccoli, cauliflower, spinach, and kale)

Frozen wild blueberries

Frozen raspberries

Frozen strawberries

Your favorite non-dairy ice cream (the cleanest you can buy, or home-made)

Frozen pesto (preferably homemade)

Equipment

When it comes to food prep, once I've got myself organized and my food stocked, I would be nothing without my equipment. For me, it all starts with a well-sharpened chef's knife and a wood cutting board that I love. But there are some other tools that take my life to the next level. Invest in this list of items and I promise, your life in the kitchen will also markedly improve.

A well-sharpened chef's knife

A good paring knife

A good small serrated knife (for cutting tomatoes)

A few great wood cutting boards

A honing steel (for repositioning your knife blades)

A whetstone (for sharpening knives)

Food processors—one large (9 cup) and one small (2 to 3 cups)

High-powered blender (my faves are Breville and Vitamix)

Silicone baking cups

Paper cupcake liners

Silicone baking mats

Baking sheets (for roasting veggies)

Glass baking dishes, large and small

Glass food-storage containers (no more plastic!)

Pots and pans that can go from the stovetop to the oven (cast iron)

Cupcake trays

An ice cream maker (not as important, but still helpful)

Mason jars of all sizes (for storing nut butters, nut milks, sauces, etc.)

Beautiful platters of all sizes and shapes (for easy serving when guests come over)

Wax paper

Parchment paper

Cellophane wrap

Foil

Plastic storage bags—big and small

The Difference Between a Steel and a Whetstone

A steel (the tool that comes with most knife sets) hones the blade by straightening it and pushing it back to the center. The edge of a knife gets pushed to either side as it's used, especially if handlers of the knife use the blade to push food from the cutting board into a bowl, pot, or pan. (You actually want to use the back of the knife to do this to protect the edge of the knife.) While honing doesn't sharpen the knife, it does reposition the blade to the center, which allows it to cut more efficiently. It is recommended that people hone their knives often; some even do so before each use.

A whetstone (or a water stone or electric knife sharpener) grinds or shaves off bits of the blade to sharpen it. You usually only have to sharpen your knives once or twice a year, depending on how often you use them. Contrary to popular belief, it is much safer to use a sharp knife than a dull one. Why? Sharper knives cut more easily through food, allowing you much more control. With a dull knife, you have to push much harder to cut through a piece of food and you are more likely to slip and cut yourself. If you do manage to cut yourself with a sharp knife (which happens all the time), the cut is more likely to be cleaner than if the knife were dull.

| *Steel* | *Whetstone* |

The Weekender Frittata (page 18)

Breakfast

This is arguably my favorite meal of the day. When I was younger, my favorite breakfast food was cereal. Sugary cereal. Lots of it. I ate that way until my mid-20s when I expanded my palate beyond the scope of your typical breakfast cereals. Since then, I've had some pretty amazing savory creations to start off my day, and I'll never go back! The Weekender Frittata (page 18) is a crowd pleaser for your next brunch, as is the Shakshuka (page 24), which seems to be making a comeback.

THE WEEKENDER FRITTATA

SERVES 4 TO 6

I had a bunch of moms coming over for a mommy group some time ago, and I wanted to prepare something delicious for them. They weren't expecting breakfast, but before I knew it, I had decided to raid my fridge and throw whatever I had on hand into a frittata. I sautéed up greens and mushrooms, oven-roasted some cherry tomatoes, and caramelized some onions. I baked all of it into a frittata, and pulled out a masterpiece that was promptly devoured by my very hungry mamas! Making frittata always works best if you have a skillet that can transfer from the stovetop to the oven, but if you don't have one, don't fret. You can simply make everything on the stove-top and then transfer everything to a bake dish.

7 to 8 tablespoons (110 ml) extra virgin olive oil (EVOO)

1 large yellow onion (thinly sliced)

1 teaspoon (5 ml) plus a pinch of sea salt

½ teaspoon (2 ml) plus a dash of pepper

1 pint (320 g) of cherry tomatoes (rinsed and dried)

1 bunch Swiss chard (roughly chopped)

1 bunch kale (any kind will do, roughly chopped)

1 cup (50 g) of shiitake mushrooms (cleaned and sliced)

12 eggs

1. Preheat oven to 375° Fahrenheit (190° C).

2. Heat 2 tablespoons (30 ml) of extra virgin olive oil (EVOO) in a large skillet over medium-low heat. (It might have to be on low depending on the strength of your flame/element.) Add in your sliced onions. Stir every 5 to 10 minutes as they caramelize. Should take anywhere from 30 to 40 minutes.

3. While the onions are caramelizing, place your cherry tomatoes on a baking sheet and drizzle with 1 to 2 tablespoons (15 to 30 ml) of EVOO, and add a pinch of sea salt and pepper. Use your hands to toss until all the tomatoes are covered. Spread out in an even layer. Bake at 375° F (190°C) for about 20 minutes or until tender.

4. While the tomatoes and onions are cooking, wash and roughly chop your Swiss chard and kale and place in a bowl. Drizzle with 1 tablespoon (15 ml) EVOO, and add a pinch each of sea salt pepper. Use your hands to massage the oil and spices into your greens and set aside.

5. Remove the caramelized onions from the pan and set aside. Then, using the same pan, heat 2 tablespoons (30 ml) of EVOO over medium-low heat. Wash and slice the mushrooms and add to the sauté for about 5 minutes or until they start to soften. Then add your greens, sautéing for another 5 minutes or so until the greens are tender. Once they are cooked down, add the onions and tomatoes back into that pan with the mushrooms and greens.

6. Break 12 eggs into a bowl and whisk with 1 teaspoon of sea salt and ½ teaspoon (2 ml) of pepper, until combined. Turn the heat down to low, and pour the eggs into the pan over the sautéed veggies. Resist the urge to stir! Let the eggs gently cook over low heat for about 5 minutes. After that time has elapsed, place your pan into the oven and bake for about 20 to 30 minutes or until set in the middle. Serve warm.

> *Note:* *If you don't have a pan that can go in the oven, simply pour your veggies into a baking dish and then cover with eggs and place directly in the oven. Bake as instructed above.*

Baking Powder Paleo Substitute

To make 1 tablespoon (15 ml) of baking powder:
Mix together 1 teaspoon (5 ml) baking soda and 2 teaspoons (10 ml) cream of tartar.

To make 1 teaspoon (5 ml) of baking powder:
Mix together ¼ teaspoon (1 ml) baking soda with ½ teaspoon (2 ml) cream of tartar.

Source: www.paleoplan.com/ingredients/baking-powder/

PALEO BANANA WALNUT BLUEBERRY PANCAKES

SERVES: 4

What kid doesn't love pancakes? And what adult doesn't remember being a kid who loves pancakes? Pancakes are for the kids in all of us, and they should be consumed, if only on special occasions. But you can put your store-bought mix away, because this recipe for paleo banana walnut blueberry pancakes will be the only pancake recipe you'll ever need again. With the crunchiness of the walnuts, the natural sweetness of the blueberries, and the soft texture of the cake itself, you'll wonder how something that tastes so good could also be so good for you—and paleo approved!

¾ cup (70 g) Bob's Red Mill Paleo Baking Flour

1 tablespoon (15 ml) arrowroot or potato starch

1 teaspoon (5 ml) baking powder

¼ cup (50 g) coconut sugar

2 tablespoons (30 ml) pure maple syrup

1 teaspoon (5 ml) vanilla extract

¾ cup (175 ml) almond milk

1 banana, sliced

Handful of blueberries

Coconut oil for cooking

Handful of walnuts

1. Whisk together the dry ingredients in a bowl (paleo flour through coconut sugar).

2. Add the wet ingredients. Stir until combined.

3. Add the sliced banana and blueberries to the batter and mix gently until combined (but don't mash the bananas).

4. Heat 1 tablespoon (15 ml) of coconut oil in a pan at medium to medium-high heat. Using a ladle, scoop out the batter and place onto the pan. Break or chop some walnuts to place over the pancake. Cook the pancake until air bubbles start to form on the top, then flip it over and cook another 1 to 2 minutes.

5. Repeat the process until all the pancakes are done. Should yield 4 medium-sized pancakes or 8 small ones.

6. Serve as is or with real maple syrup, smile as you do, and enjoy!

Shakshuka (page 24)

SHAKSHUKA

SERVES: 4 TO 6

When my husband, Ted, ran the Boston Marathon in 2015, my friend, Scott, and I flew there to support him. While Ted ran, Scott and I restaurant hopped, testing out different places we had read about or heard from locals that we needed to go to. (We are big foodies.) The day before the race, we read about this place to go for breakfast near Harvard Square, and we were told we must have the Shakshuka. This is basically a spicy tomato sauce with eggs baked into it, and it didn't disappoint. I needed to make this myself, so when I got back home to LA, I got to work recipe testing. This has easily become one of my favorite recipes! The beauty of it is that because it's a savory dish, while it's a great breakfast item, it also works well as a lunch or dinner item too.

1 to 2 tablespoons (15 to 30 ml) extra virgin olive oil (EVOO)

2 medium onions (1 chopped to medium dice, the other thinly sliced)

Half a fresh red bell pepper or 1 fire-roasted one from a jar, chopped to a medium dice

5 cloves of garlic, minced

1 teaspoon (5 ml) and a pinch of kosher salt

½ teaspoon (2 ml) ground black pepper

1 tablespoon (15 ml) fresh thyme

½ teaspoon (2 ml) ground cumin

½ teaspoon (2 ml) cayenne

½ teaspoon (2 ml) paprika

1 28-ounce (800 g) can of plum tomatoes

¼ cup (40 g) sundried tomatoes

4 eggs

4 to 5 ounces (110 to 140 g) goat cheese

Half bunch of parsley, chopped

1. Heat 1 to 2 tablespoons (15 to 30 ml) of EVOO over medium heat in an ovenproof pan. Caramelize your onions, both diced and sliced, for 30 minutes.

2. If using fresh bell pepper, add it to the onions after 30 minutes, and continue sautéing and caramelizing for another 20 to 30 minutes. If using bell peppers from a jar, add them at the same time as the sundried tomatoes (step 5).

3. Turn the heat down to low and add in the minced garlic and a pinch of salt. Sauté the garlic just until you can start to smell it—probably about 1 to 2 minutes.

4. Add the thyme along with all the other spices, tossing to combine. Let the flavors infuse together for about 5 minutes.

5. Add the can of tomatoes along with the sundried tomatoes and a jar of chopped red peppers (if not using fresh). Crush the tomatoes with the butt of your spatula into bite-size pieces.

6. Turn the heat back to medium and let the sauce simmer for about 10 to15 minutes, stirring occasionally.

7. Preheat the oven to 375° Fahrenheit (190°C).

8. Once the sauce has simmered for 10 to 15 minutes, create a divot in one section of the sauce. Crack a single egg into a small bowl, and then pour the egg into the divot. Repeat the process for all 4 eggs. Sometimes I'll add as many as 6 or 8 eggs if the pan is big enough and I have more mouths to feed.

9. Place the entire pan in the oven and let the eggs cook for about 7 to 9 minutes or until the eggs are cooked the way you like them.

10. Remove from the oven and sprinkle with generous amounts of goat cheese and parsley. Serve warm on its own or on a paleo-approved slice of toast.

LEEKS AND GREENS BREAKFAST BOWL

SERVES: 4

When I'm not drinking a smoothie for breakfast, savory is by far my most favorite way to enjoy breakfast. I recently tested this recipe for leeks and greens in a coconut milk broth, and I quickly discovered that topped with a poached egg or two, I had the makings of a ridiculously elegant, tasty, and healthy breakfast. This has quickly become a new favorite, and I think it will become the same for you and your family! This recipe easily makes enough for 4 to 5 people, so poach as many eggs as you need to top it off!

3 tablespoons (45 ml) extra virgin olive oil (EVOO)

4 large leeks, cleaned and sliced

4 cloves garlic, sliced

1 bunch of kale, stem removed and roughly chopped

1 quart (2 L) whole coconut milk

1 teaspoon (5 ml) curry powder

1 teaspoon (5 ml) sea salt

½ teaspoon (2 ml) pepper

2 eggs, poached

1. Heat the oil over medium-low heat. Sauté/sweat the leeks and garlic over low heat for about 10 minutes or until translucent. Add the kale and sauté for another 5 minutes or until wilted down.

2. Add the coconut milk, curry powder, sea salt, and pepper. Bring to a simmer and cook for about 5 minutes.

3. To serve, scoop out desired amount into a bowl and top with 2 poached eggs.

SPICED BREAKFAST SWEET POTATOES

SERVES: 4

I had friends coming over for brunch when my daughter was only a few months old, and by that time, I wasn't quite back in the swing of things. It was a win if I could get a shower in on a given day, much less actually cook myself something to eat. I don't know what I was thinking inviting people over for a meal that I was to prepare, but before the words could be retreated, my friends took me up on the offer. I decided to go simple: scrambled eggs, a beautiful green salad, and sweet potatoes. But I wanted to jazz the sweet potatoes up a little, so I added some spices, sautéed them instead of roasting them, and got myself a crowd pleasing little breakfast side! Everyone asked for seconds, and I rushed to my tattered recipe-testing book to write the recipe down before it fell out of my head (like everything else seems to since having a baby; mommy brain—it's a thing). Enjoy!

1 to 2 tablespoons (15 to 30 ml) extra virgin olive oil (EVOO)

3 to 4 small or 2 large sweet potatoes, skin on, washed and cubed

½ teaspoon (2 ml) ground black pepper

½ teaspoon (2 ml) sea salt

½ teaspoon (2 ml) ground cumin

½ to 1 teaspoon (1 to 2 ml) chili powder

1. Heat the EVOO over medium-high heat in a large skillet. Add your cubed sweet potatoes and all the spices. Toss to coat.

2. Turn the heat down to medium and cover the potatoes with a lid to let them steam and sauté for about 10 minutes or until tender. Stir them around every few minutes to make sure you don't burn the bottoms.

3. Once tender, turn your heat up to high and toss the potatoes around to brown them. Serve warm.

Tip: If you have leftovers, keep these in the fridge not only to warm up for later, but to add them to a tossed salad for extra flavor!

BREAKFAST SALAD

SERVES: 1 TO 2

I used to be pretty pure with my breakfast. Savory dishes didn't belong anywhere before noon, in my opinion. But since I stopped eating sugar, processed foods, meat, and gluten, I had to get over myself. Since then, I am not opposed to eating any meal, at any time of the day. Breakfast for dinner, dinner for breakfast—no problem. But there is a restaurant near my house that took things to the next level: a breakfast salad! I was so intrigued that I had to order it, and oh man, was it ever good! I've now started to make my own version of it, and now, you can too! Feel free to use this recipe as your guide, and add or take away whatever suits you!

2 eggs, scrambled

2 handfuls of spring mix

1 handful of spinach

½ cup (120 g) Spiced Breakfast Sweet Potatoes (page 29) or Garam Masala Roasted Butternut Squash (page 85)

½ an avocado, sliced

½ cup (25 g) sautéed shiitake mushrooms

2 tablespoons (30 ml) extra virgin olive oil (EVOO)

1 teaspoon (5 ml) balsamic vinegar

½ teaspoon (2 ml) sea salt

½ teaspoon (2 ml) pepper

1. Sauté the shiitake mushrooms in a tablespoon of EVOO, sea salt, and pepper.

2. Place all ingredients in a big salad bowl. Drizzle with the EVOO, balsamic vinegar, and pepper. Toss to combine. Enjoy!

BREAKFAST PIZZA WITH SWEET POTATO CRUST

SERVES: 2 TO 4

Here is another meal whose two words don't seem to go together: breakfast and pizza. But when I lived in Vancouver during culinary school, I went to a restaurant with a local food critic where they specialized in breakfast pizzas. Turns out, if you add eggs to a pizza, it immediately becomes breakfast! Who knew?! But since I'm not into gluten and processed grains anymore, I had to come up with a vegan crust that would serve as the base for my pizza. I adapted a recipe from one of my favorite cookbooks, *Blissful Basil*, and the results didn't disappoint! This has become a household favorite. And soon you'll see why!

I batch sweet potato pizza crust (recipe below)

I onion, thinly sliced

I batch of vegan pesto (page 149)

4 to 6 eggs (depending on how many people you're feeding)

For the sweet potato pizza crust:

3 cups (725 g) of cooked sweet potatoes (yams), cubed

1½ tablespoons (22 ml) water

½ cup (50 g) Bob's Red Mill Paleo Baking Flour

2 tablespoons (30 ml) almond meal

I tablespoon (15 ml) EVOO

I teaspoon (5 ml) apple cider vinegar

I teaspoon (5 ml) garlic powder

I teaspoon (5 ml) Italian seasoning

I teaspoon (5 ml) sea salt

½ teaspoon (2 ml) black pepper

1. Preheat oven to 400° Fahrenheit (200°C).

2. Caramelize your onions by placing them in a skillet with a tablespoon of EVOO over medium-low heat for about 30 to 40 minutes or until brown. Toss every 5 to 10 minutes to prevent burning and sticking.

3. While the onions are caramelizing, make the pizza crust. Place your potatoes in a large bowl and mash with a fork or potato masher until smooth. Add in all of the rest of the ingredients. Mix until all is combined.

4. Line a large baking sheet with parchment paper or a silicone-baking mat. Spread the "dough" on the baking sheet and—using your fingers—pat it down to about ¼ inch-(.75 cm) thick, doing your best to make the shape of a rectangle. Bake it for about 20 minutes or until the edges are golden.

5. When the crust is done, pull it out of the oven. Top it with pesto and caramelized onions. Place it back in the oven to stay warm while you make your eggs on the stove. (Turn off the oven, and let the residual heat act as a heater.)

6. Prepare your eggs any way that suits you (poached, sunny side up, over easy). Once they are done, place them on top of the pizza.

7. Serve as is or with a little bit of hot sauce!

SPIRULINA SPINACH BREAKFAST BOWL

SERVES: 1

When I was in Steamboat Springs, Colorado a few years ago, I found this amazing little restaurant on the main drag. It was all vegan except that they served eggs. I was in heaven. I ordered this amazing spirulina breakfast bowl and I went back the next morning for another one. I couldn't stop thinking about it, so I decided I had to replicate my own at home. I've come up with something close to the real thing! Enjoy!

For the broccoli:

1 cup (230 g) broccoli or broccolini

1 clove garlic

1 tablespoon (15 ml) extra virgin olive oil (EVOO)

Pinch each of sea salt and pepper

For the spinach:

1 large handful (about 2 cups/360 g) spinach

1 tablespoon (15 ml) extra virgin olive oil (EVOO)

1 clove garlic

Pinch each of sea salt and pepper

The rest:

2 eggs

½ cup (100 g) cooked quinoa

1 tablespoon (15 ml) Spirulina Pesto (page 145)

1 tablespoon (15 ml) sesame seeds

1. Sear/sauté the broccoli in EVOO and garlic on high heat for about two minutes. Sprinkle with a pinch each of sea salt and pepper and toss to combine.

2. Sauté the spinach in EVOO and garlic over medium heat until the spinach is wilted down. Sprinkle with a pinch each of sea salt and pepper and toss to combine.

3. Prepare your eggs either sunny side up or over easy.

4. Place the quinoa, broccoli, and spinach in a serving bowl. Place the eggs on top of it, and drizzle with some spirulina pesto and sesame seeds.

5. Adjust the seasoning (you may need more salt and pepper), and top with your favorite hot sauce if you'd like!

BEET AND WINTER SQUASH BREAKFAST BOWL

SERVES: 1

This bowl is another play on the Spirulina Breakfast Bowl, and it's just as delicious! But this time, instead of hues of green, we're playing around with yellow butternut squash, rich red beets, and a hint of green arugula. Sometimes I think this bowl might just be too pretty to eat, but my stomach always gets the best of me as I devour the whole bowl and wish for seconds.

½ cup (90 g) roasted butternut squash, small diced

1 tablespoon (15 ml) extra virgin olive oil (EVOO)

1 teaspoon (5 ml) balsamic vinegar

Pinch of sea salt

Pinch of pepper

½ cup (90 g) diced, cooked golden or red beets

1 handful (about 1 cup) arugula

2 eggs

1 tablespoon (15 ml) Beet Pesto (page 147)

1 tablespoon (15 ml) pine nuts, toasted

1. Remember, I like to keep roasted veggies in my fridge at all times. If you haven't already prepared your butternut squash, prepare it according to the instructions (step #5 on page 88).

2. Place the EVOO, balsamic vinegar, sea salt, and pepper in a bowl and whisk to combine. Add your beets and arugula into the bowl and toss to combine. Set aside.

3. Prepare your eggs sunny side up or over easy.

4. To serve, smear a tablespoon of beet pesto along the entire bottom of the serving bowl. Place your veggies over top, and then top with your 2 eggs. Drizzle with another bit of beet pesto and you're ready to feast!

Optional: If you have some basil oil on hand (page 151), feel free to drizzle that over top of it as well.

Grapefruit, Strawberry, Mango Guacamole (page 45)

Appetizers and Snacks

I've always been more of a grazer than a big meal type of gal. I remember on special occasions, while my mom was preparing dinner in the kitchen, she would always set out a plate of cheese, crackers, and pâté for us to nosh on. And when we would get home from school, there was always a plate of something to snack on: bananas with PB and a chocolate chip on top, saltine crackers with PB and J on top, or whatever my mom concocted and had on hand that day. As I have aged, my appetizers and snacks have taken a more sophisticated turn to match my more complex and discerning palate. I think you will find that any one of the recipes that follow will serve as a new favorite for you, your family, and your future guests. Enjoy!

WARM SPINACH ARTICHOKE DIP WITH CASHEW RICOTTA CHEESE

SERVES: 4 TO 6

When I was a kid, my friend's mother used to make this ridiculously creamy (read dairy-filled) crab dip with crackers. It was warm, it was rich, and I'm sure it was very, very bad for me. But I didn't care. Her mom used to make a bowl just for me because I loved it so much. But since I don't do dairy anymore (and I almost never eat seafood), I had to find a solid contender to substitute this heavenly dip. This dip absolutely does the trick. Hands. Down. It's warm and creamy without being heavy, and you actually feel good after eating it. Score!

For the dip:

- 1½ tablespoons (22 ml) extra virgin olive oil (EVOO)
- ½ cup (75 g) red onion, diced
- 2 cloves of garlic, minced
- 1 12- to 14-ounce (400 g) can of artichokes, roughly chopped
- 1 pound (450 g) frozen spinach, thawed, rinsed, and drained
- 1 teaspoon (5 ml) sea salt
- ½ teaspoon (2 ml) ground black pepper
- 1 cup (90 g) cashew ricotta cheese (recipe below)
- 1 teaspoon (5 ml) apple cider vinegar

For the cashew ricotta:

- 1½ cups (225 g) raw cashews, soaked overnight and then strained and rinsed
- The juice from 1 lemon (about 2 tablespoons/30 ml)
- ½ to 1 tsp (2-5 ml) sea salt
- ¼ to ¾ (60-75 ml) cups water

1. Blend all the cashew ricotta ingredients together in a food processor until smooth.

2. For the dip, heat up EVOO over medium heat. Sauté the onions until translucent (about 5 minutes), then add garlic and sauté for another minute.

3. Add the artichokes, spinach, salt, and pepper to the sauté, tossing around just until the spinach begins to warm up.

4. Add in the cashew ricotta, and toss to combine. Finish it off with a teaspoon of apple cider vinegar. Toss until mixed through.

5. Serve warm with veggies, chips, or crackers. Enjoy!

CASHEW CHEESE WITH ROASTED DATES

SERVES: 6 TO 8

As someone who grew up eating a lot of meat, I get a little insecure when I invite people over for dinner parties. My mom always had a plate of cold cuts out for everyone to enjoy before dinner, or some kind of pâté or cheese dish. But since I don't eat that way, I kind of force my guests into my vegetarian/vegan ways. But I like to cook with a carnivore in mind, so when I'm coming up with recipes, I make sure to include everything a meat-eater would want: good texture, delicious taste, and hearty enough to be filling. I tested this appetizer out on a few dinner guests at Christmas time a few years ago (all meat eaters), and I couldn't have been more pleased: the entire plate was gone long before dinner was ready to be served! You'll soon find out why.

2 cups (250 g) raw cashews, soaked for 4 hours or overnight

2 tablespoons (30 ml) fresh lemon juice

1 tablespoon (15 ml) nutritional yeast

1 cup (175 g) whole dates, pitted

1 tablespoon (15 ml) extra virgin olive oil (EVOO)

1 teaspoon (5 ml) sea salt

½ teaspoon (2 ml) pepper

For the cheese:

1. Blend the soaked cashews, lemon juice, and nutritional yeast together in a food processor for 10 to 12 minutes or until smooth.

2. Chill the "cheese" in the fridge directly in the food processor for about an hour or until cool and thick.

3. While the "cheese" is chilling, line a 4-inch pan with wax or parchment paper so that the paper covers the entire pan and comes out the sides, too.

4. When the "cheese" is cool, use a spatula to scoop it into the paper-lined pan, pressing down and molding it into the contours of the pan. Place the pan in the fridge, and allow the cheese to cool in the mold for at least four hours.

5. When ready to serve, take the "cheese" out of the fridge and place a cheese board on top of the pan. Holding the pan and the cheese board together, flip them over, and remove the pan from the "cheese," peeling away the wax or parchment paper. You will be left with a perfectly molded, spreadable cashew cheese!

For the dates:

1. To make the dates, line a baking sheet with parchment paper. Remove the pits from the dates, place the dates on the baking sheet, and drizzle with EVOO, sea salt, and pepper. Serve warm, alongside your "cheese." Encourage your guests to smear some cashew cheese on top of a date for optimal flavor!

GRAPEFRUIT, STRAWBERRY, MANGO GUACAMOLE

SERVES: 4

Is there anything better than a bowl of guac on a hot summer's day? Okay, maybe a glass of refreshing iced tea (see the drink section for plenty of those recipes), but guac just seems like a staple. Everyone has a guacamole recipe. This one takes my favorite basic guacamole recipe and turns it up a notch. By adding fruit to the mix (not too much), it not only is incredibly pleasing to the taste buds, but it adds color, which is incredibly pleasing to the eyes and makes your guests think you are the world's best chef (which, of course, you are, right?).

3 to 4 ripe avocados, halved

Juice of ½ a lemon

Juice of 1 lime

2 to 3 tablespoons (30 to 45 ml) red onion, finely chopped

½ teaspoon (2 ml) sea salt

½ teaspoon (2 ml) pepper

1 mango, ripe and chopped into chunks

1 ruby red grapefruit, sectioned

4 to 5 strawberries, diced

1. Place avocados in a bowl with the lemon and lime juice, salt and pepper. Mash until smooth (or chunky, if you prefer chunky guac).

2. Add the onions, mangoes, ruby red grapefruit, and strawberries to the bowl. Stir to combine. Test the seasonings and adjust as necessary. Serve and enjoy!

GRAINLESS GRANOLA

SERVES: 8

One of the most heartbreaking discoveries in my journey to health has definitely been that granola is not as healthy as we thought it was. I used to love eating coconut yogurt with fresh granola on top, but once I actually did the math and realized how calorie heavy and nutrient deficient most granola recipes are, my heart sank. But it didn't take me long to figure out how to give a not-so-healthy meal a facelift! And this recipe doesn't disappoint. Expect light sweetness, a crunchy texture, and a nutrition-packed recipe that you can sprinkle on top of your yogurt without a hint of guilt!

4 tablespoons (60 ml) coconut oil

1 tablespoon (15 ml) ground cinnamon

1 tablespoon (15 ml) nutmeg

½ teaspoon (2 ml) ground cloves

½ cup (125 ml) maple syrup

1½ cups (115 g) shredded coconut

1 cup (135 g) sunflower seeds

1 cup (135 g) pumpkin seeds (pepitas)

1 cup (170g) whole almonds

½ cup (60 g) slivered almonds or chopped pecans

½ cup (60 g) dried dark cherries (optional)

½ cup (60 g) raisins (optional)

1.   Preheat oven to 325F (160° C). Line a large baking sheet with parchment paper or a silicone baking mat.

2.   Heat the coconut oil in a pan over medium heat until melted. Add in the spices and syrup and gently heat until all is incorporated and the mixture begins to simmer. Set aside.

3.   Place the shredded coconut, seeds, and nuts in a large bowl, and toss to combine. Pour the syrup mixture over it, and toss again.

4.   Place the mixture in an even layer on the parchment-paper-lined baking sheet. Bake in the oven for 30 minutes, tossing with a spoon every 10 minutes to ensure nothing burns.

5.   After 30 minutes, add in the dried fruit (if you're using it) and toss around. Bake for another 5 minutes.

6.   Let it cool. Store in an airtight container at room temperature for up to a week.

SWEET PEA HUMMUS

SERVES: 4 TO 8

I have to tip my hat to my friend Doria for this recipe. Every time I go to her house for a party, she always serves a version of this dip. She serves it with gluten-free garlic crackers, which—though incredibly flavorful—aren't the healthiest. So, I usually grab a carrot stick or piece of celery to dip instead. This dip has a really neat green color that adds a little flare to any table, and it makes for a great, healthy snack, too!

1 10-ounce (284 g) package of frozen peas, thawed

2 cups (170 g) chickpeas, cooked

¼ cup (60 ml) tahini

3 cloves of garlic, minced

Juice of 2 lemons

1 teaspoon (5 ml) sea salt

½ teaspoon (2 ml) black pepper

Add all the ingredients into a food processor and blend until smooth. Serve with veggies.

CHOCOLATE PROTEIN BALLS

SERVES: 4 TO 8

Life is fast. There are a lot of moving pieces. And since becoming a mother, time slips away from me even quicker than I can write this sentence. I don't always take the time to make a nutritious meal, and sometimes I admittedly just charge right through my day without sitting down to eat. Having these protein balls on hand is a lifesaver when I'm absolutely starving and about to reach for something bad for me. They are not only packed with protein and other good nutrients (depending on the quality of your protein powder, of course), but they also taste like dessert. It's a win-win!

½ cup (60 g) vegan chocolate protein powder (whichever one you like best)

½ cup (40 g) shredded coconut

½ cup (60 g) chopped pecans

½ cup (115 g) almond butter (Homemade is best—page 140—but you can use store-bought.)

1 tablespoon (15 ml) coconut oil, melted

1 to 3 teaspoons (5 to 15 ml) water, depending on how dry the dough is

1. Combine the dry ingredients in a bowl and stir. Add the wet ingredients, starting with one teaspoon of water. Use a fork to mix it around, and then use your hands when the fork doesn't cut it anymore! If the dough is still too dry to form a ball, add another ½ teaspoon (2 ml) of water, mixing (and adding water as needed) until you get a consistency like cookie dough.

2. Once you reach the right consistency (this could take anywhere from 1 to 3 or even more teaspoons (5 to 15 ml) of water), take a tablespoon measurement and roll out your balls!

3. Store in an airtight container in the fridge for up to one week.

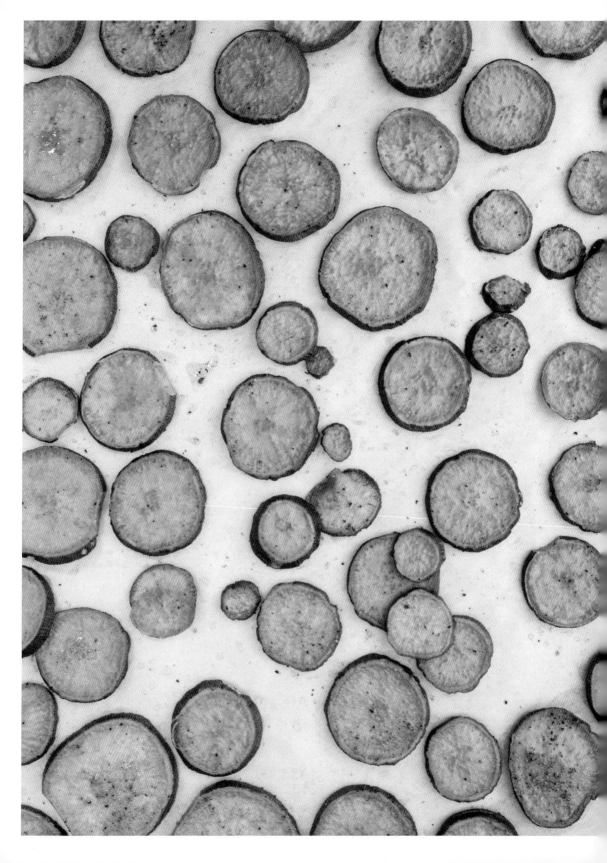

SWEET POTATO CHIPS

SERVES: 4

I got on the spiralizer train last year when a friend gave me one as a gift. I tested it out that very night with the sweet potatoes I had on hand. (I always have sweet potatoes, or rather, yams, on hand.) I have to tell you: these "chips" didn't make it from the pan to the table. I stood over the oven and ate them all myself! My husband only heard about them and how delicious they were, because there weren't any left by the time he got home. Be sure to keep them in the oven long enough so that they get crispy! Some ovens are hotter than others, so play around with the temperature a few degrees up or down to make sure you get just the right crunch!

3 to 4 medium-sized sweet potatoes (yams will do too),
    washed and unpeeled

2 to 3 tablespoons (30 to 45 ml) extra virgin olive oil (EVOO)

½ teaspoon (2 ml) sea salt

¼ teaspoon (1 ml) pepper

1. Preheat oven to 400° Fahrenheit (200° C).

2. Use a spiralizer to thinly slice your potatoes.

3. Place them in an even layer on a baking sheet. Drizzle with EVOO, sea salt, and pepper.

4. Bake for 20 minutes or until crisp and baked through.

Powerhouse Salad (page 62)

Salads and Soup

If you were to visit my home on any given night of the week, chances are that you would find me noshing on a salad. Same goes for lunch too. It's just so easy to whip up some greens and top them with some yummy accoutrements and a great dressing or to manipulate any vegetable and turn it into a salad. I swear my husband and I eat about twelve salads a week between the two of us, maybe more. And because of how easy they are to prepare, and how well they keep in the fridge and/or freezer, soups are a close second. I'm quite picky about the quality of the ingredients that go into my food, so I find when it comes to soup, it's always better to make it myself. Besides, it's much more cost effective: you can make a batch of soup that will last for many meals for the same price as you might pay for a single serving in a restaurant, and all in a single pot. Now that's healthy cooking made easy!

GRILLED VEGGIE SALAD WITH PESTO

SERVES: 4 TO 6

As far as I'm concerned, the world can never have enough pesto. I always have a batch or two made and stored in the freezer for a quick, elegant, and tasty meal in a pinch. I also always have veggies on hand because they are chalked full of nutrients and flavor, and they can be manipulated and used in so many creative ways! If you like to grill, this recipe for grilled veggie salad will have your family and guests oooo-ing and ahhh-ing at your mad culinary skills. Enjoy this recipe hot off the grill or cool in the fridge, and enjoy the cold leftovers the following day!

1 pound (450 g) cherry tomatoes

1 pound (450 g) zucchini, sliced ½-inch thick lengthwise

4 portobello mushrooms, cleaned and whole

5 to 6 cups (1200 g) arugula

1 small head of broccoli, broken into large florets

1 small head of cauliflower (or half a large one), broken into large florets

½ small head of radicchio

¼ cup (30 g) hazelnuts, roughly chopped

A lot of extra virgin olive oil (EVOO), to grill all the veggies

Lots of sea salt and pepper

1 batch of pesto (see page 149)

1. Preheat oven to 375° Fahrenheit (190° C).

2. Heat your indoor or outdoor grill to high temperature.

3. Place the cherry tomatoes on a baking sheet and drizzle with 1 tablespoon (15 ml) of EVOO, ½ teaspoon (2 ml) of sea salt, and ½ teaspoon (2 ml) of black pepper. Bake for 20 minutes or until tender. Set aside.

4. Prepare the rest of your veggies: Place 5 tablespoons (75 ml) of EVOO, 1 teaspoon (5 ml) of sea salt, and 1 teaspoon (5 ml) black pepper in a bowl. Whisk until combined. Starting with the zucchini and then one veggie group at a time after that, place into the marinade and toss to combine. Using a pair of tongs, place the zucchini on the grill. Grill for about 2 minutes, then turn and grill another 2 minutes. Repeat with the rest of your veggies. You don't want the veggies to be cooked through too much because you want them to have great grill marks on them! They will cook a bit, to be sure. But no soggy veggies here please!

5. Once all your veggies have been grilled, slice them into the size you desire, and place them all in a bowl. Add the cherry tomatoes and about half of your pesto. Toss to combine. Adjust the seasonings and add more pesto if needed. Serve warm or cold.

YOUR NOT-SO-EVERYDAY SUPER SALAD

SERVES: 2

One thing that I always have on hand in my house is salad. The rule is that whoever takes the last of it must replace it immediately. If it weren't for salad, my husband and I would surely go hungry. When we are busy working from home, we just want to be able to throw some things in a bowl, drizzle it with some dressing, toss, and go on about our work. Our salads change from day to day depending on what's in the fridge: hard boiled eggs, leftover roasted veggies from the night before, legumes (we still eat those in limited amounts in this house), nuts, seeds, avocado. You get the picture! Here is a basic recipe, but please feel free to make it your own based on whatever is available in your fridge!

I handful spring mix greens

I handful arugula or spinach (or another handful of spring mix)

Half an avocado, sliced

I tablespoon (15 ml) hemp seeds

I tablespoon (15 ml) sesame seeds

Half a roasted red pepper (from a jar), small diced

I handful of whole almonds

2 hard boiled eggs, roughly chopped

Half a date, roughly chopped

Leftover roasted veggies (if you have any on hand; if not, it will still be good)

I teaspoon (5 ml) balsamic vinegar

3 tablespoons (45 ml) extra virgin olive oil (EVOO)

Pinch of sea salt

Pinch of pepper

Place all ingredients in a large salad bowl. Drizzle with vinegar, oil, salt and pepper. Toss to combine. Enjoy!

FRENCH CANADIAN LENTIL SOUP

SERVES: 6 TO 8

I am from Montreal, but I'm not actually French Canadian. I feel like I am, since I moved there when I was a wee tyke (I was 4), and I certainly grew up eating foods native to that province. (Think lots of poutine and maple syrup-covered snow. Seriously.) Thankfully, there are some other French Canadian dishes that are actually quite healthy. This lentil soup bears the French Canadian name, but it's actually not a traditional French Canadian dish. I just based the recipe on a dish that was French Canadian, and I liked the way it sounded, so... Voila! I'm happy to report that the flavor profile does bear resemblance to a lot of savory French Canadian dishes. It's also warm and comforting, which is the exact kind of meal one needs to get through the very rough Quebec winters. Enjoy this on a cold day, and prepare for it to warm you through and through.

6 tablespoons (90 ml) extra virgin olive oil (EVOO)

1 to 2 leeks, quartered and thinly sliced

1 medium-large yellow onion, small diced

4 bay leaves

3 to 4 large carrots, small diced

2 to 3 stalks of celery, small diced

4 teaspoons (20 ml) garlic powder

1 teaspoon (5 ml) dried oregano

1 teaspoon (5 ml) turmeric

1 teaspoon (5 ml) ground black pepper

1 cup (240 ml) white wine

1 pound red lentils (uncooked)

1 to 2 tablespoons (15 to 30 ml) nutritional yeast (optional)

1 teaspoon (5 ml) sea salt

5 to 6 cups (1½ liters) filtered water

Hot sauce (optional)

1. Heat up your EVOO over medium heat in a large soup pot. Sauté the leek, onions, and bay leaves for about 5 minutes or until translucent. Add the carrot and sauté for another 3 to 5 minutes. Then add the celery and sauté for another 3 to 5 minutes.

2. Turn up the heat to high, and stir in the spices. Sauté for about another minute.

3. Once hot enough, pour in the wine. It should sizzle when you add it in. Stir the concoction so as to get the brown little bits off the bottom of the pot.

4. Stir in the rinsed lentils, nutritional yeast (if using), and the water. Bring it to a boil, and then reduce to a simmer. Cook covered for about 20 minutes, or until the liquid is almost fully absorbed.

5. Remove the bay leaves. Taste and season with more salt and pepper if need be. Voila!

6. Enjoy on its own or with some hot sauce—so good!

POWERHOUSE SALAD

SERVES: 4 TO 6

My husband and I own and operate a yoga studio in Malibu. One year, I decided to host a salad competition for the holidays. Originally I wanted it to be a dessert bake-off, but that didn't seem to fit the bill for a yoga studio, so salad it was! A surprising amount of people participated (read: more than just myself) and got really creative! I based this recipe off the winner who prepared something similar. The other salads were great, but I licked the bowl clean on this one. I think you will too!

For the Brazil nut Parmesan:

1 cup (120 g) Brazil nuts

1 teaspoon (5 ml) minced garlic

½ teaspoon (2 ml) sea salt

You can also use ½ cup (45 g) store-bought vegan Parmesan cheese.

For the butternut squash and caramelized onions:

2 cups (350 g) baked butternut squash (or sweet potatoes/yams if squash is not in season)

1 teaspoon (5 ml) sea salt

½ teaspoon (2 ml) black pepper

½ teaspoon (2 ml) garam marsala

1 to 2 tablespoons (15 to 30 ml) extra virgin olive oil (EVOO)

1 medium-sized onion

1 tablespoon (15 ml) extra virgin olive oil (EVOO)

For the salad:

8 cups mesclun mix (600 g)

2 to 3 cups (350 to 500 g) kale, stemmed, chopped

1 teaspoon olive oil

1½ cups (240 g) cold cooked quinoa (can substitute with cauliflower rice)

½ cup chopped fresh parsley

½ cup (75 g) pomegranate seeds and their juices

1 medium sized granny smith apple, chopped but not peeled

½ cup (75 g) cubed jicama

¼ cup (30 g) toasted walnuts

1 scallion, chopped

2 tablespoons (30 ml) ginger, finely grated using a microplane zester

Juice of 1 lemon (more if the lemon isn't very juicy)

2 tablespoons (30 ml) extra virgin olive oil (EVOO)

½ teaspoon (2 ml) ground cinnamon

1½ teaspoons (7 ml) sea salt

½ teaspoon (2 ml) ground black pepper

6

1. Preheat the oven to 375° Fahrenheit (190°C).

2. To make the Brazil nut Parmesan "cheese" place the Brazil nuts, garlic, and sea salt into a food processor and pulse until you get a parmesan cheese-like texture. Use half of it in this recipe, and store the rest in an airtight container in the fridge for up to one week. Use it on any of your savory dishes throughout the week!

3. To bake the butternut squash, first peel, seed, and chop a small butternut squash into ½-inch (1.5 cm) cubes. Place on a sheet pan and drizzle with sea salt, pepper, garam marsala, and EVOO. Bake for 30 minutes or until tender.

4. Caramelize your onion by first thinly slicing it. Heat 1 tablespoon (15 ml) of EVOO in a pan over medium-low heat. Place the onions in the pan, and toss to coat. Keep stirring every 10 minutes for about 40 minutes or until the onions are golden brown.

5. Massage the kale with the olive oil. Combine in a bowl with the salad ingredients, butternut squash, and caramelized onions, along with the Brazil nut Parmesan. Toss. Enjoy the magical flavors as they infuse your body with nutrients and delight!

WHITE BEAN, WINTER SQUASH, DILL, ROASTED VEGGIE SALAD

SERVES: 4 TO 6

This salad was a happy accident. I didn't have much in the way of food prepared one night, but I was itching to make something healthy for dinner. I was in no mood to head out to the store, so I scoured the pantry and fridge and came up with this recipe. It's a bit time consuming if you don't already have the veggies roasted and the almond tuna prepared, so you might want to keep that in mind so you can prepare those things ahead of time. But fear not: if you haven't pre-prepared things, you can still make it. It might take a little longer, but I promise you, it will be more than worth it in the end!

For the salad:

½ head of cauliflower

½ head of broccoli

1 cup (180 g) white beans, cooked

1 cup (200 g) chickpeas, cooked

1 cup (225 g) vegan almond tuna (see step 3 on page 110)

¼ cup (30 g) toasted pecans

1 handful arugula

1 cup roasted butternut squash (125 ml), (see page 85 for roasting instructions only)

1 handful fresh parsley, washed, dried and finely chopped

1 handful of fresh dill, washed, dried and finely chopped

1 teaspoon (5 ml) sea salt

½ teaspoon (2 ml) black pepper

For the dressing:

1 tablespoon (15 ml) Dijon mustard

2 tablespoons (30 ml) red wine vinegar

3 tablespoons (45 ml) extra virgin olive oil (EVOO)

½ teaspoon (2 ml) honey or maple syrup

1 teaspoon (5 ml) sea salt

½ teaspoon (2 ml) black pepper

1. Preheat oven to 375° Fahrenheit (190°C).

2. To roast the broccoli and cauliflower, cut each vegetable into bite-sized pieces. Place on their own individual pans, and drizzle with EVOO, sea salt, and pepper. Bake at 375° Fahrenheit (190°C) for about 20 minutes or until browned and cooked through.

3. Place your roasted veggies, along with the rest of your ingredients in a bowl and drizzle with dressing. Toss to combine.

PURPLE POTATO SALAD

SERVES: 6

I don't eat a lot of potatoes, but whenever I pass by the purple potatoes at the farm-ers' market, I can't resist. Plus—there has to be some good nutrition in that vibrant purple color, don't you think? That said, I tend to eat this salad in small portions so as not to overdo it on carbs. But it's a lovely alternative to the traditional potato salads that have adorned the tables of many a Canadian and American picnic table since the dawn of modern time! You couldn't find a healthier potato salad if you tried.

1 bag of small purple potatoes (approximately 1.5 lbs or 680 g)

1 handful fresh dill, chopped

1 handful fresh parsley, chopped

1 handful chives, chopped (or 2 green onions, chopped)

1 cup (100 g) purple cabbage, finely chopped

¼ cup (30 g) pine nuts, toasted

1 15-ounce (425 g) can of white beans

1 to 2 tablespoons (15 to 20 ml) extra virgin olive oil (EVOO)

Sea salt and pepper to taste

1.   Preheat oven to 375° Fahrenheit (190°C).

2.   Cut the potatoes in half and place them on a sheet pan. Drizzle with EVOO, sea salt, and pepper (about ½ teaspoon/2 ml each). Toss them with your hands to ensure all the potatoes are covered in oil, salt, and pepper, and then roast them at 375° Fahren-heit (190°C) for about 25 minutes or until tender.

Once the potatoes are ready, let them cool for 10 minutes and then place them in a big bowl with the rest of the ingredients. Add another tablespoon of EVOO, toss, and taste. See if it needs more sea salt and pepper. If the flavor is flat, add another ½ teaspoon (2 ml) of sea salt. Toss. If still flat, add another ½ teaspoon.

3.   Serve hot or cold and enjoy the purple goodness!

> *Note: Modern paleo thought is that potatoes that have been cooked and cooled provide a source of resistant starch that promotes healthy gut flora. They also don't count as a carbohydrate source, because once cooled, potatoes have an altered carbohydrate structure, thereby rendering them resistant to normal digestion.*

SUMMER SALAD WITH CHAMPAGNE VINAIGRETTE

SERVES: 2 TO 4

I love cooking by the season. Don't get me wrong, there are recipes that I eat all year long. But there are other recipes that I only tend to pull out when the weather changes. This recipe is one of my go-to summer recipes. By the time fall rolls around, I've eaten enough of this salad that I wait until the next summer to enjoy it all over again. It's fresh and crunchy, a little bit sweet, and a touch salty. It's basically summer in a salad.

For the salad:

- 1 handful butter lettuce, chopped
- 2 handfuls mixed greens
- 6 to 7 strawberries, washed and chopped
- 1 nectarine, sliced
- 1 avocado, sliced
- 2 tablespoons (16 g) cucumber, peeled and thinly sliced
- 2 tablespoons (16 g) red onion, thinly sliced
- 1 handful sugar snap peas, chopped
- 1½ tablespoons (15 g) toasted pecans
- 16 toasted hazelnuts, chopped
- A pinch each of sea salt and pepper

For the vinaigrette:

- 2 tablespoons (30 ml) champagne vinegar
- 6 tablespoons (90 ml) extra virgin olive oil (EVOO)
- 1 teaspoon (5 ml) Dijon mustard
- 1 teaspoon (5 ml) honey
- 1 clove garlic, minced
- ½ teaspoon (2 ml) dried thyme
- ¼ teaspoon (1 ml) sea salt
- ¼ teaspoon (1 ml) pepper

Place all salad ingredients in a bowl, and drizzle with 2 tablespoons (30 ml) of vinaigrette. If you need more dressing, add another tablespoon. Enjoy!

BLUEBERRY BRUSSELS SPROUTS SALAD WITH LEMON VINAIGRETTE

SERVES: 2

I used to go to a place in Santa Monica called M Street Kitchen (formerly Le Grande Orange) for their Brussels sprout salad. They basically made a salad out of the leaves of Brussels sprouts rather than using traditional salad leaves, which was amazing! Ever since then, when I'm feeling like mixing things up a little (we eat salads daily in my house), I break out this recipe. Be mindful, though. Peeling off the leaves of Brussels sprouts isn't exactly quick. Have patience, have good company (your significant other, a good podcast, some nice music), and enjoy the journey!

For the salad:

1 pound (450 g) fresh Brussels sprouts

½ cup (120 g) fresh blueberries

¼ cup (35 g) slivered almonds, toasted

¼ cup (35 g) hemp seeds

For the dressing:

2 tablespoons (30 ml) fresh lemon juice

6 tablespoons (90 ml) extra virgin olive oil (EVOO)

1 clove garlic, minced

½ teaspoon (2 ml) oregano

½ teaspoon (2 ml) sea salt

½ teaspoon (2 ml) pepper

1 teaspoon (5 ml) Dijon mustard

1 teaspoon (5 ml) honey or maple syrup

1. Trim the ends off the Brussels sprouts. Using a paring knife, peel the leaves off of each sprout and place the leaves in a salad bowl. Repeat until you have a bowl filled with leaves! This may take a while, so put on some fun tunes or a great podcast and enjoy the process!

2. Put the blueberries, toasted almonds, and hemp seeds into the bowl with the sprout leaves. Set aside and make your dressing.

3. Place all the ingredients for the dressing into a jar with a tight-fitting lid. Close the lid and shake until thoroughly combined. You can also whisk together the dressing ingredients in a bowl.

4. Drizzle half the dressing over the salad and toss. If you find you need more dressing, add another drizzle and keep tossing and adding dressing until you get the desired amount. This could mean using the entire batch if you like a lot of dressing.

KALE SALAD WITH SPICY ALMOND DRESSING

SERVES: 4 TO 6

As you probably already guessed, I do a lot of recipe testing and also a lot of restaurant food tasting. It's where I get inspired to think outside the box, and where I get to take a break from being the chief meal officer of my household and let someone else cook for me for a change. One of my favorite restaurants is M Cafe. They have something for everyone: carnivore, vegans, pescatarians, and fruitarians alike! I had their kale salad with spicy peanut dressing a few years back, and though I don't normally eat peanut butter anymore, I couldn't resist. And it was soooo good! If you're down with peanuts, go ahead and use the recipe as is. If not, substitute it with almonds and almond butter, and you'll still love the results!

I bunch of organic kale, stemmed, and roughly chopped

I medium red onion, caramelized

¼ cup (35 g) sliced almonds, roughly chopped

For the dressing:

½ cup (160 g) unsalted smooth almond butter, preferably homemade (page 140)

2 tablespoons (30 ml) tamari (gluten-free soy sauce) or coconut aminos

2 tablespoons (30 ml) rice vinegar

1½ tablespoons (22 ml) honey

I clove garlic, minced

I teaspoon (5 ml) fresh ginger, minced

A pinch of sea salt

¼ teaspoon (1 ml) red pepper flakes

¼ cup (60 ml) hot water (plus more if the dressing is too thick)

1. Roughly chop the kale, and then put it in a food processor in batches to finely chop it.

2. Place all dressing ingredients in a blender and blend until smooth.

3. Place kale, almonds, and onions in a bowl, and drizzle with dressing. Toss and serve!

ARUGULA AND WINTER SQUASH SALAD

SERVES: 2

When my husband did his second Leadville 100-mile mountain bike race in Colorado a few years ago, we went to this amazing restaurant in Denver called Root Down. They served up a salad that was so beautiful in its presentation and equally as pleasing to my palate. I recreated it in my test kitchen, and the results didn't disappoint. This recipe isn't so much about cooking as it is about plating. So be prepared to gather recipes that have been littered throughout this book and put them together to create this masterpiece.

For the salad:

2 handfuls arugula

I tablespoon (30 ml) extra virgin olive oil (EVOO)

I teaspoon (5 ml) balsamic vinegar

I teaspoon (5 ml) sea salt

½ teaspoon (2 ml) pepper

For the beets:

3 small golden beets, cooked and small diced

I tablespoon (15 ml) extra virgin olive oil (EVOO)

½ teaspoon (2 ml) sea salt

½ teaspoon (2 ml) pepper

For everything else:

I tablespoon (15 ml) beet pesto (page 147)

I teaspoon basil oil (5 ml) (page 151)

2 tablespoons (30 ml) almond ricotta (store-bought: I like the Kite Hill and Treeline brands)

I cup (125 g) roasted butternut squash (see page 85 for roasting instructions only)

2 tablespoons (50 g) hazelnuts, roughly chopped and toasted

1. Toss the arugula in EVOO, vinegar, salt, and pepper. Set aside.

2. Toss the beets in EVOO, salt, and pepper. Set aside.

3. Take a large plate and smear beet pesto horizontally along the bottom of the plate with a spoon. (See picture.)

4. Divide your chopped beets in half, and place a pile of them on top of the pesto on either side of the plate. Drizzle basil oil in both directions along the plate.

5. Place the tossed arugula perpendicular to the pesto and down the plate in a neat line. Top it with butternut squash on either side of the arugula. Top with your ricotta and hazelnuts, drizzle some more basil oil, and enjoy!

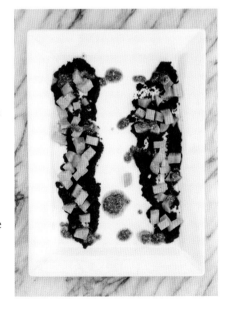

HEIRLOOM CAPRESE SALAD WITH GRILLED PEACHES

SERVES: 2

Since we are on an elegant salad roll, let's keep it going, shall we? When peaches and heirloom tomatoes are in season, so is this salad. The recipe is super easy to prepare, and you won't believe how something so simple could taste—and look—so good. I love preparing this for dinner guests, or bringing it as a side to add to a potluck during a summer BBQ. It always dazzles the crowd!

For the tomatoes:

2 large heirloom tomatoes cut into ¼-inch (0.6 cm) wedges

1 tablespoon (15 ml) extra virgin olive oil (EVOO)

1 tsp (5 ml) balsamic vinegar

1 tsp (5 ml) sea salt

½ tsp (2 ml) black pepper

For the peaches:

1 large peach, cut into ¼-inch (0.6cm) wedges

1 tablespoon (15 ml) extra virgin olive oil (EVOO)

1 teaspoon (5 ml) balsamic vinegar

1 teaspoon (5 ml) sea salt

½ teaspoon (2 ml) black pepper

For the arugula:

1 handful of arugula

1 teaspoon (5 ml) balsamic vinegar

1 teaspoon (5 ml) sea salt

½ teaspoon (2 ml) black pepper

Other ingredients:

2 teaspoons (10 ml) basil oil (page 151)

1 tablespoon (15 ml) almond ricotta (store-bought: I like the Kite Hill and Treeline brands)

1. Preheat your grill to high heat.

2. Toss the tomatoes in EVOO, vinegar, sea salt, and pepper. Set aside.

3. Toss the arugula in EVOO, vinegar, sea salt, and pepper. Set aside.

4. Toss the peaches in EVOO, vinegar, sea salt, and pepper. Grill the wedges on either side for about 2 minutes each.

5. To plate the salad, take a large plate (or small serving plates), and drizzle the bottom of the plate with basil oil. Get creative! There is no wrong way to do this!

6. Top with arugula. Then line the tomatoes and peaches along the middle of the bed of arugula, alternating them: tomato, peach, tomato, peach, etc.

7. Drizzle with a bit more basil oil, and sprinkle with almond ricotta. Enjoy!

CHICKPEA SOUP WITH PESTO

SERVES: 6

When I'm out of ideas and time, this recipe is a sure go-to. It's a one-pot wonder, which is music to any busy person's ears (especially a mother's, let me tell you), and it feeds at least 5 or 6 people. It's hearty, tasty, and best of all, it takes almost no time to prepare. Serve it as is, or with a dollop of the basic pesto from page 149. Season it with salt and pepper and enjoy!

3 tablespoons (45 ml) extra virgin olive oil (EVOO)	2 15-ounce (425 g) cans chickpeas, drained and rinsed
2 medium onions, small diced	1 quart (4 cups/1 liter) veggie stock
1 tablespoon (15 ml) dried thyme	4 cups (1 liter) filtered water
6 cloves garlic, minced	2 teaspoons (10 ml) sea salt
1 28-ounce (800 g) can plum tomatoes and their juices	1 teaspoon (5 ml) ground black pepper

1. Heat the oil in a pan over medium heat. Add in the onions and dried thyme. Let them sauté for about 5 minutes or until translucent.

2. Add your garlic and toss for about 30 to 60 seconds or until fragrant. Then add in your can of plum tomatoes. Using the tip of your silicone spatula, roughly "chop" the tomatoes into reasonable sized pieces. Let the mixture cook down for about 5 minutes.

3. Add your chickpeas. Then, using a potato masher, squish the chickpeas down so that 50 to 75% of the chickpeas are squished, and the remainder remain whole. (Don't worry—it doesn't have to be an exact science. We're just going for texture here).

4. Turn the heat up to high and add in your stock and water. Add in your sea salt and pepper. When it comes to a boil, turn the heat down to medium and let the soup simmer for about 20 minutes.

5. Adjust the seasonings, and remove from heat.

6. To serve, spoon a ladle or two of soup into a bowl. Place a dollop of pesto on top, and stir it around until it's combined. Adjust the seasonings with salt and pepper, and enjoy!

7. This soup is AMAZING as leftovers because you can just heat up what you want in a pot over the stove, and it's ready in 5 minutes! So, feel free to double the recipe!

Truffled Mac and (Goat) Cheese
(page 114)

As a child, if it wasn't frozen chicken nuggets with sweet and sour dipping sauce or some kind of hot dog or hamburger with ketchup for dinner, I wasn't much interested. Thankfully, I have traded in my desire for processed food into one for healthy, wholesome, farm-to-table options. Admittedly it takes a little bit more time to prepare, but I have found that the reward more than outweighs the extra effort. Use your spinach artichoke dip to stuff a portobello mushroom for an elegant meal fit for any guest (page 82). Or put together a pasta-free lasagna using butternut squash for a crowd-pleasing spin on an Italian classic (page 86). Whatever the case, I think these recipes will help open your eyes to all the possibilities a main dish can provide.

Mains

SPINACH ARTICHOKE-STUFFED PORTOBELLO MUSHROOMS

SERVES: 4

It's always nice when you can mix and match recipes, don't you think? Especially when you can take an appetizer and make it a main meal. This recipe does just that. For vegetarians, we have to get creative with our protein sources because there are only so many eggs a person can eat! That's why I love using portobello mushrooms. They are a powerhouse of nutrients—protein included. And best of all, they are accessible and easy to work with. So, load up your plate with these stuffed beauties tonight!

1 tablespoon (15 ml) Dijon mustard

3 tablespoons (45 ml) extra virgin olive oil (EVOO)

1 teaspoon (5 ml) sea salt

½ teaspoon (2 ml) black pepper

4 portobello mushrooms

Warm spinach artichoke dip (page 40)

1. Preheat oven to 425° Fahrenheit (220°C).

2. Whisk the Dijon mustard, EVOO, sea salt, and pepper in a small bowl until combined.

3. Remove the stems and place the mushrooms on a baking sheet or dish lined with parchment paper or a silicone baking mat. Brush or drizzle the mushrooms with the oil mixture. Bake for 20 minutes.

4. Remove from the oven. Place a dollop of the warm dip into each of the mushroom caps and return to the oven for 5 minutes.

GARAM MASALA ROASTED BUTTERNUT SQUASH

SERVES: 4 TO 6

When butternut squash is in season, I'm a happy camper. It reminds me of autumn on the east coast. (I'm from Montreal.) Living now in always-sunny L.A. (I'm not complaining), I sometimes get nostalgic for cozy blankets and that crisp smell of fall in the air. Insert roasted veggies here. It's amazing what roasting vegetables can do. This technique really and truly is the only reason I started eating vegetables in my early twenties. It draws out the sugars of whatever veggie you're roasting, and those sugars begin to brown and caramelize on the bottom of the pan. That's why it's really important to use a well-used (read: beat-up) old baking sheet for this and the other roasted veggie recipes in this book. And with this particular recipe, the garam masala adds a new level of flavor to the party. Try it out and see for yourself!

1 medium-size butternut squash, peeled and cubed

2 to 3 tablespoons (45 ml) extra virgin olive oil (EVOO)

½ teaspoon (2 ml) sea salt

½ teaspoon (2 ml) pepper

1 teaspoon (5 ml) garam masala

1. Preheat oven to 375° Fahrenheit (190°C).

2. Place the butternut squash on a baking sheet. Toss with EVOO, sea salt, pepper, and garam masala. Use your hands to ensure all the pieces are coated. Spread out in a single layer.

3. Bake for about 30 minutes or until tender.

BUTTERNUT SQUASH ALFREDO LASAGNA WITH BRAZIL NUT PARMESAN

SERVES: 4 TO 6

Like any lasagna, I'll admit, this recipe is a little bit more involved. It takes some preparation to prepare all of the moving parts. But I promise you it is well worth the effort. It also makes a pretty substantial portion, so you can feed an entire family and have leftovers for a day or two afterward. Best practice? Double the recipe so you can freeze one to pull out of the freezer in a pinch on the next I'm-too-busy-to-cook night!

Ingredients (for lasagna) in order of preparation:

- 1 medium butternut squash, sliced in ¼-inch pieces
- 2 tablespoons (30 ml) extra virgin olive oil (EVOO)
- 1 teaspoon (5 ml) sea salt
- ½ teaspoon (2 ml) black pepper
- 2 cups (475 ml) vegan Alfredo sauce (see below)

- 1 5-ounce (140 g) box of arugula or spinach (works out to about 4 to 5 cups)
- 1½ to 2 cups (340 to 450 g) cashew ricotta
- ½ cup (115 g) Brazil nut Parmesan

For the Alfredo sauce:

- 1 cup (125 g) macadamia nuts
- ¼ small yellow onion, chopped small dice
- 1 teaspoon (5 ml) garlic, minced

- ½ cup (120 ml) unsweetened almond or non-dairy milk
- ¼ teaspoon (1 ml) nutmeg
- ½ teaspoon (2 ml) black pepper
- 1 teaspoon (5 ml) sea salt

For the cashew ricotta:

- 1½ cups (190 g) raw cashews, soaked overnight
- Juice of 1 lemon (about 2 tablespoons)

- ½ to 1 teaspoon (2 to 5 ml) sea salt
- ¼ to ¾ cup (60 to 175 ml) water

For the Brazil nut Parmesan:

- 1 cup (125 g) Brazil nuts
- 1 teaspoon (5 ml) garlic, minced

- ½ teaspoon (2 ml) sea salt

1. Preheat oven to 375° Fahrenheit (190°C).

2. Add all the ingredients for the Alfredo sauce into a blender or food processor, and blend until smooth. Set aside.

3. Take the cashews you've soaked overnight and rinse and strain them. Then combine all the ingredients for the cashew ricotta in a blender, adding just ¼ cup (60 ml) of water to start. Blend until you get a paste/ricotta-like texture. If you find it's too thick, add another ¼ cup (60 ml) of water. Once you get the desired consistency, taste to see if it needs more salt. If not, you're done!

4. Place all the ingredients for the Brazil nut Parmesan in a mini food processor and pulse until you get the consistency of Parmesan cheese. Set aside.

5. To prepare the butternut squash "lasagna noodles," place the sliced squash in a glass baking dish. (You may need to separate them into two dishes.) Drizzle with EVOO, sea salt, and pepper. Toss to combine and spread out in an even layer (as even as possible). Bake at 375° Fahrenheit until tender for about 20 to 30 minutes. Remove from the oven and set aside to cool. Turn the oven temperature down to 350° Fahrenheit (180°C) in preparation for baking the lasagna.

6. It's time to layer your lasagna!* Take a glass baking dish and spread some Alfredo sauce along the bottom. Next cover the sauce with a layer of some of your cooked butternut squash slices. Take a handful of arugula and/or spinach and spread it over the butternut squash.

7. Drizzle another layer of Alfredo sauce over the greens. Follow this with some cashew ricotta cheese and then add another layer of butternut squash "noodles."

8. Follow with the rest of your greens, then the rest of your Alfredo sauce and the last of your cashew ricotta cheese.

9. Seal up your lasagna by layering the rest of your butternut squash. Lastly, sprinkle ½ cup of the Brazil nut Parmesan to top it all off!

10. Bake your lasagna at 350° Fahrenheit (180°C) for about 20 to 30 minutes or until warmed through and the "Parmesan" begins to brown.

*Layers:

Alfredo sauce

Butternut squash "noodles"

Arugula or spinach

Alfredo sauce

Cashew ricotta cheese

Butternut squash "noodles"

Rest of the greens

Rest of the alfredo sauce

Rest of the cashew ricotta cheese

Rest of the butternut squash

Brazil nut Parmesan sprinkled on top

Spaghetti Squash with Pesto and Lentil Meatballs (page 92)

SPAGHETTI SQUASH WITH PESTO AND LENTIL MEATBALLS

SERVES: 6

As a half-blooded Italian, pasta is part of my history. I consumed more than my fair share of it up until my early twenties, so when I decided to cut out most gluten 10 years ago, I was worried about having to give up my Italian birth right! But I need not have worried, because not only did I find a plethora of other recipes to keep me distracted from missing my pasta, but I also discovered the almighty "pasta" substitute: spaghetti squash. The first time I worked with it, my husband walked into the kitchen and saw me dragging my fork along the cooked flesh and remarked, "Wow! Neat trick!" He honestly thought the fork was some kind of magical tool that created pasta! There is indeed something magical about the way Mother Nature made this wonderful squash. It's almost like she knew the gluten-free movement was coming, and she wanted us to be prepared. You can substitute this squash in place of any regular pasta and serve it with any of your usual pasta sauces. I served this to a hungry bunch of male carnivores at Christmas dinner one year, and all I heard were complaints of being stuffed. Mission accomplished.

For the spaghetti squash pasta:

- 3½ tablespoons (50 ml) extra virgin olive oil (EVOO)
- 1 medium-size onion, sliced
- 1 medium-size spaghetti squash
- 1 pound (450 g) cherry tomatoes
- 1 to 2 teaspoons (5 to 10 ml) sea salt
- 1 teaspoon (5 ml) ground black pepper
- 1 handful of fresh basil leaves, roughly chopped
- ¼ cup (30 g) raw or roasted cashews, roughly chopped

For the lentil meatballs:

- 2 tablespoons (30 ml) flax seed meal
- 6 tablespoons (90 ml) water
- 1 to 2 teaspoons (5 to 10 ml) EVOO
- 1 medium onion, chopped small dice
- 4 cloves garlic, minced
- 2 cups (250 g) cooked lentils
- ¼ cup (30 g) cashews
- ¼ cup (30 g) sunflower seeds
- ½ cup (75 g) fresh parsley, roughly chopped
- 1 teaspoon (5 ml) dried thyme
- 1 teaspoon (5 ml) dried oregano
- ¼ teaspoon (1 ml) sea salt
- ½ teaspoon (2 ml) pepper

THE ACCIDENTAL PALEO

1. Preheat oven to 400° Fahrenheit (200°C).

2. Heat 1 tablespoon (15 ml) EVOO in a skillet over medium-low heat. Sauté your onions in the skillet for about 40 minutes or until browned. Stir every 5 to 10 minutes to avoid burning.

3. In the meantime, cut the spaghetti squash in half lengthwise, and scrape out the seeds. Drizzle ½ teaspoon (2 ml) of EVOO onto each of your spaghetti squash halves, massaging the oil into the flesh. Place the two squash halves—flesh side down—in a ceramic or glass baking dish. Fill the dish with water so that it comes up between ½ to 1 inch (1¼ to 2⅓ cm). Set aside.

4. Place your cherry tomatoes on a sheet pan and drizzle with 1 tablespoon (15 ml) EVOO, ½-1 teaspoon (2 to 5 ml) sea salt, and ½ teaspoon (2 ml) ground black pepper. Using your hands, toss to ensure that all the tomatoes are coated in oil.

5. Place both the tomatoes and the squash in the oven at the same time. Roast the tomatoes for 25 minutes and the squash for 30 to 45 minutes or until tender. (You will know the squash is ready when you stick a fork in the skin and it comes out without any resistance.)

6. Once the squash is ready, scrape a fork along each half to dislodge the "spaghetti," and place in a large glass bowl. Add in the roasted cherry tomatoes, caramelized onions, fresh basil, and cashews. Add in ½ teaspoon (2 ml) of ground black pepper, ½ teaspoon (2 ml) of sea salt, and 1 tablespoon (15 ml) of EVOO. Toss, taste, and adjust seasonings if need be.

7. To make the lentil balls, place the flax seed meal in a bowl with 6 tablespoons (90 ml) of water. Stir it around and place it in the fridge to gel.

8. Heat up your EVOO over medium-high heat. Sauté your onions in the pan until translucent (about 10 minutes). Add the garlic and sauté for another minute. Turn the heat off and set aside.

9. If using raw lentils, rinse them and then bring 4 cups (1 liter) of water to a boil. Add 1¼ cups (150 g) of lentils. Reduce the heat and let simmer with the lid tilted for 20 to 25 minutes or until tender. Place cooked lentils into a food processor along with the cashews, sunflower seeds, parsley, and spices. Pulse until half the mixture forms a paste and half the mixture is still coarse. (You're trying to get the consistency of ground meat.)

10. Pour the lentil mixture into the pan with the onions and garlic. Add the flax seed meal gel, and stir to combine.

11. It's time to make your "meat" balls! Using an ice cream scoop (if you have one), scoop out some lentil "meat" and form a ball. Place it on a baking sheet lined with either a silicone mat or parchment paper. Repeat the process until you finish off the mixture.

12. Bake the "meat" balls at 400° Fahrenheit (200°C) for 15 to 20 minutes, or until browned on the bottom.

13. Serve over pasta or spaghetti squash with pesto (page 149) or your favorite pasta sauce, or serve them any way you'd like!

Veggie Bowl with
Chipotle Mayo (page 96)

VEGGIE BOWL WITH CHIPOTLE MAYO

SERVES: 2

This is one of those recipes that is great for dinner in a hurry. I tend to keep veggies on hand, and I especially like to roast or sauté them so they are ready in the fridge for me to put a meal together in a pinch. This bowl does just that. It's kind of an everything-but-the-kitchen-sink veggie bowl because you're in charge. I make suggestions below, but ultimately, you get to decide what veggies to put in this bowl based on what you have on hand or what you like. Just be sure to keep chipotle mayo in the fridge and ready to use, and you'll always be able to build a nutritious, hearty, tasty meal in no time.

½ to I cup (65 to 125 g) oven-roasted sweet potatoes

2½ tablespoons (37 ml) extra virgin olive oil (EVOO)

½ teaspoon (2 ml) and a pinch of black pepper

I teaspoon (5 ml) and a pinch of salt

I cup (125 g) oven-roasted cauliflower (page 132)

I cup (125 g) caramelized oven-roasted broccoli (page 98)

½ cup (65 g) purple cabbage

I tablespoon (15 ml) of your favorite chipotle mayo

1. Cut 2 large sweet potatoes into ½-inch cubes. Drizzle with 2 tablespoons (30 ml) of EVOO, black pepper, and sea salt. Bake for 20 to 25 minutes, or until tender.

2. Using a large serving bowl, arrange I cup (125 g) of roasted cauliflower, I cup (125 g) of roasted broccoli, and I cup (125 g) of roasted sweet potatoes next to each other.

3. Slice the purple cabbage, and in a separate bowl, drizzle it with ½ tablespoon (7 ml) of EVOO, a pinch of sea salt, and a pinch of pepper. Toss to combine. Sprinkle the now-lightly dressed purple cabbage over the top of the veggies in your serving bowl.

4. Drizzle I to 2 tablespoons (15 to 30 ml) of chipotle mayo, serve, and enjoy!

Mark Sisson's Homemade Primal Kitchen Chipotle Lime Mayo

For the Primal Kitchen Homemade Classic Mayo:

1 egg yolk

1 teaspoon (5 ml) lemon juice

¼ teaspoon (1 ml) Dijon mustard

1 teaspoon (5 ml) cold water

¼ teaspoon (1 ml) salt

¾ cup (175 ml) avocado oil

For the chipotle lime sauce in the mayo:

1 teaspoon (5 ml) lime juice

1 teaspoon (5 ml) chives, chopped

1 teaspoon (5 ml) garlic powder

1 tablespoon (15 ml) adobe sauce

½ cup (125 ml) homemade mayo

Whisk together the egg yolk, lemon juice, mustard, water, and salt until frothy.

Whisking constantly, pour in the avocado oil very slowly, only a drop at a time, until the mayo begins to thicken. Once this happens, you can add the oil in a thin stream, whisking until completely combined.

Mix the lime juice, chives, garlic powder, and adobe sauce into ½ cup (125 ml) of the mayo.

Homemade mayo can stay fresh up to a week in the refrigerator, but usually tastes best if eaten within a few days.

CARAMELIZED OVEN-ROASTED BROCCOLI

SERVES: 4

Roasting. You know I love it, and if you haven't already discovered this amazing cooking technique, you're soon going to love it too. Sometimes I will take an entire head of broccoli and cauliflower, roast it, put it in a bowl, and drizzle it with some of my favorite hot sauce—that will be my dinner. This may not work for all of you, especially if you have done a particularly hard workout near the end of the day. Just remember the old rule: eat breakfast like a king, lunch like a prince, and dinner like a pauper. You don't have to be crazy like me and just eat veggies for dinner; feel free to use this recipe as a delicious side to whatever else you're making.

I head of broccoli

2 to 3 tablespoons (30 to 45 ml) extra virgin olive oil (EVOO)

Pinch of sea salt

Pinch of pepper

1.   Preheat oven to 375° Fahrenheit (190°C).

2.   Chop broccoli into small bite-size pieces and place on a baking sheet, preferably an older, beat up one (this helps with the caramelization). Drizzle with EVOO, salt, and pepper, and toss with your hands until each piece is evenly coated.

3.   Bake for 20 minutes or until browned on the bottom.

COLLARD GREEN-WRAPPED BLACK BEAN BURGERS

SERVES: 8

I still enjoy a good bean burger, and this is one of my favorite recipes. It's chock-full of nutrients and has a great flavor and texture. If you're not into eating a lot of legumes, you can swap out the beans in this recipe for shiitake or portobello mushrooms. Top these with chipotle mayo (page 97), and wrap them in a collard leaf or romaine lettuce, and you've got a meal fit for a king.

¼ cup (30 g) pumpkin seeds

½ cup (65 g) sunflower seeds

2 large carrots, grated

½ red pepper, finely chopped

1 tablespoon (15 ml) parsley

½ teaspoon (2 ml) ground cinnamon

½ teaspoon (2 ml) ground cumin

½ teaspoon (2 ml) ground coriander

½ teaspoon (2 ml) chili powder

½ teaspoon (2 ml) garlic powder

¼ teaspoon (1 ml) cayenne

1 teaspoon (5 ml) kosher salt

¼ teaspoon (1 ml) ground black pepper

¼ cup (27 g) ground flax seed meal

2 15-ounce (425 g) cans of black beans

1 tablespoon (15 ml) extra virgin olive oil (EVOO)

1 bunch of collard greens or romaine lettuce (as wraps)

Optional burger fixings:

Red onion

Pickles

Avocado

Mustard

Ketchup

1. Preheat oven to 325 Fahrenheit (160°C).

2. Blend the pumpkin and sunflower seeds in a food processor until coarsely chopped.

3. Add in the carrots, red peppers, parsley, spices, salt, pepper, flax seed meal, and ¾ of the canned black beans. Process together.

4. As it's blending together, add in your EVOO.

5. Once completely blended, remove from the food processor (be careful of the blade!) and place into a bowl. Mix in the remaining whole black beans.

6. Grease a non-stick baking sheet. Make patties using a ½ cup (120 ml) scoop measurement. They should be no more than ½-inch to ¾-inch thick (1¼ to 2 cm) so they bake evenly. Place the patties 1 inch (2⅓ cm) apart on the baking sheet. If you find your hands are sticking too much, wet your hands with water before making each patty.

7. Bake for 30 to 40 minutes, turning them over halfway through.

8. Serve on a collard green wrap along with some avocado, mayo, mustard, ketchup, and any of your other favorite burger fixings!

MANGO, SWEET POTATO, AVOCADO SUSHI ROLLS

SERVES: 4

I learned the basics of rolling sushi a few years ago. It could not be easier! Don't be intimidated like I was! You don't even need a sushi-rolling mat if you don't have or want one (though you can order them online for as little as $5). You can just use a piece of paper and a piece of plastic wrap. It's that easy! This particular recipe is a summer favorite of mine because the mango and the avocado are so refreshing. Enjoy it as an appetizer or as a main meal, depending on how hungry you are.

2 sweet potatoes

2 tablespoons (30 ml) extra virgin olive oil (EVOO)

1 teaspoon (5 ml) salt

½ teaspoon (2 ml) black pepper

2 cups (200 g) cooked quinoa or cauliflower rice

6 to 10 nori sheets

2 tablespoons (30 ml) spicy mayo or chipotle mayo

2 teaspoons (30 ml) rice wine vinegar

2 mangoes, cut into strips

2 avocados, cut into strips

A handful of sesame seeds

Small bowl of water

Optional: **Serve with tamari sauce or coconut aminos and wasabi**

1. Preheat the oven at 375° Fahrenheit (190°C).

2. Cut the sweet potatoes into long strips (think french fries). Drizzle with 2 tablespoons (30 ml) of EVOO, 1 teaspoon (5 ml) of salt, and ½ teaspoon (2 ml) of black pepper. Bake for 30 minutes. Cook the quinoa according to package instructions. If using cauliflower rice, chop up 2 cups (140 g) of cauliflower and rice it in a food processor. It doesn't have to be cooked.

3. Place a sushi rolling mat on a cutting board. Top it with a matching size piece of plastic wrap. Place the nori sheet on top of the plastic wrap.

4. Mix 2 tablespoons (30 ml) of your favorite spicy mayo along with the rice wine vinegar into the quinoa or cauliflower rice and toss until combined. Cover the nori sheet with the quinoa or cauliflower rice in a single layer, making sure you leave an inch (2.5 cm) on either side of the sheet free, as well as an inch (2.5 cm) at the top of the sheet.

5. Place the sweet potatoes, mangoes, and avocadoes in a single row about ⅓ the way up the nori sheet. Sprinkle with a dusting of sesame seeds.

6. Make your first roll by lifting up the rolling mat and squeezing the nori sheet over the veggies. Make another roll, squeezing as you go. Before you make your final roll, wet the 1-inch piece at the top of the nori sheet that you left free with water, then finish your roll. Continue rolling your sushi until you have used up all your sweet potatoes, mangoes, and avocadoes

7. To serve, either cut the rolls into pieces or eat the rolls whole. Serve with tamari (gluten free soy sauce) or coconut aminos, and wasabi if you dare.

Makes for a great healthy and nutritious snack, lunch, or light dinner!

EASY LENTIL DAL

SERVES: 6

I loooooove Indian food. Like, love it. And when I go out for Indian food, I put my nutritional priorities on the backburner because I know there are a lot of oils and other ingredients that don't sit well with me. For the nights when I'm craving this kind of food but am not willing to deal with the stomachache that inevitably follows, I break out this recipe. I know, I know—it's a legume. But it's a quick, healthy, and hearty meal that will feed a single person or a large family, and it's tasty and clean.

3 tablespoons (45 ml) coconut oil

1 teaspoon (5 ml) ground turmeric

1 teaspoon (5 ml) ground cumin

2 medium yellow onions, sliced

3 to 4 cloves garlic, minced

2 to 3 tablespoons (30 to 45 ml) fresh ginger, minced

1 pound (2 cups) (450 g) uncooked red lentils

1 14-ounce (400 g) can of coconut milk (full fat)

1 quart (4 cups/1 liter) vegetable stock

1 large handful of fresh cilantro leaves and stems, roughly chopped

1 teaspoon (5 ml) sea salt

½ teaspoon (2 ml) ground black pepper

3 to 4 handfuls of spinach

1. Heat the coconut oil over medium heat. Add turmeric and cumin and brown for 1 minute. Add the onions and sauté for 5 to 6 minutes or until translucent and soft.

2. Add the garlic and ginger. Sauté for 30 to 60 seconds (or until fragrant). Add the lentils and toss. Then add the coconut milk, vegetable stock, and cilantro. Simmer on medium heat until the lentils are cooked (about 20 minutes).

3. Once the lentils are cooked, add your salt and pepper. Then add your spinach. Begin with one handful, toss until wilted, and then add another handful. Continue in this manner until all the spinach has been added, tossed, and wilted.

4. Taste to see if you need to adjust the seasonings. Serve warm.

WEEKNIGHT VEGGIE CURRY

SERVES: 4

I love the versatility of a good curry dish. This is my go-to curry, the one I make while my husband is feeding my daughter dinner, and I have only 10 minutes to make the whole thing happen. It's so quick and easy to make, and it makes quite a substantial amount. So, it can feed a large family, or it can be stored in the fridge as leftovers for a few more meals. Everybody wins!

3 tablespoons (45 ml) coconut oil

1½ tablespoons (22 ml) fresh ginger, minced

1 small yellow onion, medium diced

4 small cloves of garlic, minced

2 teaspoons (10 ml) sea salt

½ teaspoon (2 ml) black pepper

1½ tablespoons (22 ml) curry powder

1 teaspoon (5 ml) ground ginger

½ teaspoon (2 ml) turmeric

1 tablespoon (15 ml) garam masala

3 14- to 15-ounce (425 g) cans of coconut milk (full fat)

½ cup (120 ml) vegetable stock

4 medium to large carrots, sliced ¼-inch (0.6 cm) thick

1 head broccoli, chopped

½ head cauliflower, chopped

1. Melt the coconut oil in a large saucepan over medium heat. Add in the ginger and onions, and sauté for about 5 to 10 minutes or until translucent. Add in the garlic and cook for another minute.

2. Add all the spices and stir to combine. Then add the coconut milk and veggie stock. Stir to combine, and turn up the heat so that it comes to a simmer.

3. Once simmering, add the veggies. Toss to combine. Cover with a lid and cook on medium-low heat until veggies are tender but still a bit crunchy (about 3 to 7 minutes).

4. Serve as is or with a bit of quinoa.

STUFFED ACORN SQUASH

SERVES: 4

Since becoming a vegetarian, I have developed a pretty intimate relationship with the winter squash. Acorn squash and I in particular have become best buds. I love baking it and stuffing it with whatever I have on hand, and this recipe represents one of many of such creations. When my very meat-eating father was visiting from Montreal a few years ago, he was subjected to my cooking (lest he wanted to cook his own meat, which he didn't). I served him this recipe on his first night here, and he was so surprised both by how good it was and by how full he was that he asked me for the recipe. Now he cooks this at home with my mother on the nights when they don't eat meat. I love it when the student becomes the teacher. You're welcome, Dad!

2 whole medium acorn squashes

1 cup (180 g) uncooked quinoa, rinsed

1 cup (240 ml) water

1 cup (240 ml) veggie stock

1 large handful of fresh spinach

¼ cup (30 g) pine nuts

¼ cup (30 g) cashews

1 handful of chopped fresh parsley

½ cup (65 g) sundried tomatoes

1 teaspoon (5 ml) sea salt

½ teaspoon (2 ml) ground black pepper

Drizzle of extra virgin olive oil (EVOO)

1. Preheat oven to 400° Fahrenheit (200°C).

2. Poke holes in the acorn squash with a fork in a few places, piercing the skin. Place the squash on a baking sheet, whole, and bake for 40 to 50 minutes, or until tender.

3. While the squash is baking, make your quinoa. Cook it according to the instructions on the package, which should tell you to use 2 cups (475 ml) of water per 1 cup (180 g) of quinoa. Simply substitute 1 cup of water (475 ml) with 1 cup (475 ml) of veggie stock.

4. When the quinoa is done, stir in the spinach right away so that the steam wilts it down. Toss until wilted down. Then add in your nuts, parsley, tomatoes, and spices. Set aside.

5. Once the squash is tender, remove them from the oven. Using an oven mitt, carefully cut them in half. Remove the seeds, and place the squash halves in a baking dish, skin side down. Drizzle some EVOO on top of them, and sprinkle them with some sea salt and pepper. Then fill the squash with your quinoa mixture, just to the brim.

6. Bake for another 5 minutes, and serve warm.

VEGAN TUNA-STUFFED SWEET POTATOES

SERVES: 4

One of the things that was hard for me to give up when I went vegetarian was tuna. I used to love tuna salad, especially tuna melts. Technically, as a vegetarian (but more pescatarian), I can still eat fish. But tuna is much too high in mercury for my liking, so I'm happy to keep it on the no-eat list. But it doesn't mean I don't crave it! I looked for a vegan tuna recipe for a while before combining a few to come up with this one. And I have to say—it really hits the spot. I've used this "tuna" to stuff a sweet potato as a main meal here, but you can feel free to use this "tuna" recipe in any way that suits you. Add a little mayo and/or mustard to make a "tuna" salad, serve it as a salad nicoise, or make a tuna melt—whatever moves you!

4 medium sweet potatoes

4 tablespoons (90 ml) coconut oil

½ cup (65 g) almonds, raw, soaked for 4 hours

½ cup (65 g) cashews, raw, soaked for 4 hours

1 15-ounce (425 g) can chickpeas

½ red onion, small diced

1 celery stalk, chopped

½ (2 ml) teaspoon turmeric

½ (2 ml) teaspoon garlic powder

1 teaspoon (5 ml) sea salt

½ teaspoon (2 ml) pepper

Juice of 1 lemon

A handful of parsley, roughly chopped

1. Preheat the oven to 400° Fahrenheit (200°C).

2. Wash and dry the potatoes. Poke them randomly with a knife and place on a baking dish or sheet. Bake the potatoes for 30 to 40 minutes or until tender when poked with a fork.

3. To make the "tuna," pulse the nuts in a food processor for about 5 to 10 seconds, just enough to break up the nuts. Add the chickpeas and pulse again for 5 seconds, just to break up the chickpeas. Finally, add the rest of the ingredients, and pulse until chunky, but combined (another 5 to 10 seconds).

4. You can serve the "tuna" like this, or you can feel free to add the usual suspects: Dijon mustard, mayonnaise (the vegan kind if you're vegan)—or whatever you want!

5. Remove the potatoes from the oven. Cut them open down the center, and place 1 tablespoon of coconut oil on top of each potato until it melts. Top each potato with a cup of the "tuna," serve, and enjoy!

Note: *This recipe calls for soaked almonds and cashews. Recommended soaking time is 4 hours.*

VEGETARIAN STUFFED PEPPERS

SERVES: 4 TO 6

One of my mother's specialties growing up was her stuffed peppers. She used to stuff them with minced meat, of course, and top them with her famous tomato sauce. I loved them. I have trouble digesting meat (which is why I stopped eating it), but I didn't want to say goodbye to stuffed peppers completely! So, I came up with a vegetarian stuffing. And though it doesn't taste exactly like my mother's original stuffing, it certainly packs a punch and stands on its own.

4 to 6 whole bell peppers (red, orange, or yellow), halved and seeded

2 to 4 (30 to 60 ml) tablespoons extra virgin olive oil (EVOO)

2½ cups (500 g) cooked wild rice (about 1 cup uncooked)

1 cup (200 g) cooked quinoa (can replace with cauliflower rice)

4 large dates, chopped

1 yellow squash (use green zucchini if you can't find yellow), diced

½ cup (65 g) chopped walnuts

½ to 1 cup (50 to 100 g) feta cheese

1 handful chopped parsley

1 teaspoon (5 ml) sea salt

½ teaspoon (2 ml) ground black pepper

1. Preheat oven to 400° Fahrenheit (200° C).

2. Place the halved peppers skin side down in a baking dish. Drizzle with 2 tablespoons (30 ml) of EVOO, salt, and pepper, and rub the oil into the peppers. Pour about 1 cup of water into the bottom of the dish so the peppers don't burn in the oven.

3. Place the rice, quinoa, dates, squash, walnuts, feta, salt, and pepper into a bowl. Drizzle with about 2 tablespoons (30 ml) of EVOO. Toss to combine.

4. Stuff your peppers with the rice mixture. (Don't be afraid to over stuff them—anything that falls onto the bottom of the baking dish will cook and be delicious by itself.) Depending on the size of your peppers, you will have a lot of leftover stuffing. This is okay! It's great to have on hand in the fridge to eat as a side dish or to toss into a green salad to make it heartier. You can also stuff a few more peppers if you have them on hand. You decide!

5. Cook the peppers for about 30 minutes or until they are tender. Serve warm and enjoy!

TRUFFLED MAC AND (GOAT) CHEESE (DAIRY AND GLUTEN-FREE)

SERVES: 6

This is a definite cheat, my friends! I make this recipe once a year because even though it's dairy and gluten-free, it's still quite heavy. But we should all live a little from time to time! And rather than cheat with a greasy pizza or Philly cheesesteak, why not cheat with something a lot healthier? I based this recipe off a dish that I had at a vegetarian restaurant in Santa Barbara that, unfortunately, is no longer there. I have to say, I look forward to the one time each year that I make this for myself or my guests! It's like Christmas in my mouth!

THE ACCIDENTAL PALEO

½ cup (90 g) cauliflower rice, pre-made or homemade, uncooked

1 cup (180 g) quinoa, uncooked

2 tablespoons (30 ml) extra virgin olive oil (EVOO)

1 small onion, small dice

2 garlic cloves, minced

¾ cup (95 g) cashews, soaked for 1 to 2 hours and then drained before use

1½ (7 ml) teaspoon sea salt

½ (2 ml) teaspoon ground black pepper

¼ (60 ml) cup almond milk (or other milk substitute)

½ to 1 cup (50 to 100 g) goat cheddar, grated

1 handful of parsley, chopped

Optional: 1 tablespoon (15 ml) truffle oil

1. Preheat your broiler on high.

2. If making your own cauliflower rice, place 1 cup of chopped cauliflower into a food processor and pulse until you have "rice." Next cook your quinoa according to the instructions on the box. Set the cauliflower rice and quinoa aside.

3. Sauté your onion in 1 tablespoon (15 ml) EVOO over medium heat for 15 minutes or until translucent. Add in your minced garlic near the end and let that sauté for about a minute. Set aside.

4. In a food processor, place your drained cashews, along with the warm onions and garlic, salt, pepper, and almond milk. Blend until smooth. (You may want to scrape down the sides of the bowl halfway through.)

5. In a pot that is oven safe (i.e., no rubber or plastic handle), combine your quinoa and cauliflower rice. Add half the grated goat cheddar to the pot and mix until it melts. (Your quinoa should still be on the warmer side. If you're using cooled, cooked quinoa, then just mix in the cheese and don't worry about it melting.) Pour the cashew mixture over it along with a handful of chopped parsley, the rest of your EVOO, and your truffle oil, if you're including it. Stir until all is properly combined. Taste to see if it needs any seasonings to be adjusted (more salt, pepper, oil, etc.).

6. Once the seasoning is the way you like it, smooth out the top and sprinkle the remaining cheese on top of the quinoa/cauliflower rice. Place it under the broiler until it melts and starts to brown. This could take anywhere from 5 to 15 minutes, depending on your broiler.

7. Serve warm. Feel free to eat it as is, or to dress it up with some hot sauce, more truffle oil, or anything your heart desires!

Note: This recipe calls for soaked cashews. Recommended soaking time is 2 hours.

SUNDRIED TOMATO COLLARD GREEN WRAPS

SERVES: 4 TO 6

Living in the heart of Malibu with a somewhat restrictive diet, I don't exactly have very many restaurant choices around me. I know, I know. I live in Malibu. I have nothing to complain about. True enough, but sometimes I really don't feel like cooking, so it's nice to have somewhere close to grab a bite that suits my diet and taste buds. There is a place across the street from me that has some grab-and-go vegan meals, and one such meal is a version of this recipe. I decided to try to make it myself one day, and the result was amazing. Behold a refreshing, filling, healthy vegetarian wrap for your next lunch!

1 medium to large onion

1 tablespoon (15 ml) extra virgin olive oil (EVOO)

½ cup (25 g) sundried tomatoes

3 dates

1 head organic collard greens

½ cup (120 ml) vegan pesto (page 149)

1 cup (125 g) raw cashews

¼ (1 ml) teaspoon salt

4 tablespoons (60 ml) fresh lemon juice

½ cup (120 ml) water

1 cup (182 g) organic red cabbage, sliced

1 organic (182 g) red pepper, sliced

1 organic (182 g) cucumber, peeled and sliced long ways

1 handful organic fresh parsley

1 handful organic fresh basil

1. Begin by caramelizing your onions if you don't already have some on hand. To do this, thinly slice one medium to large onion. Heat up 1 tablespoon (15 ml) of EVOO on medium heat. Add the onions to the pan, toss to combine, and turn down the heat to low. Cook on low for 30 to 40 minutes, tossing every 5 to 10 minutes until the onions are brown and caramelized.

2. While the onions are caramelizing, make the sundried tomato paste by placing ½ cup of sundried tomatoes and 3 dates together in a food processor. Blend until smooth.

3. For the cashew sour cream, blend the raw cashews, salt, lemon juice, and water in a food processor until smooth. Set aside.

4. Put your wrap together by cutting off half the spine of one your collard green leaves. Starting with one leaf, place a tablespoon each of the pesto, sundried tomato paste, and cashew sour cream. Next add a few strips of each of the vegetables and herbs on the top half of the leaf (where the spine is still intact).

5. Flip up the bottom of the collard leaf (where the spine has been removed) and roll it like a burrito. Continue with the rest of your collard greens until you have all of your wraps made! Serve as is or with your favorite dipping sauce!

SHIITAKE LEEK SAUTÉ

SERVES: 2 TO 3

I was never much into mushrooms when I was younger (or anything healthy, really), but now that I've discovered all the different kinds of mushrooms on the market, I'm hooked! I especially love shiitakes. Sometimes I'll just sauté them in olive oil and add them to my salads, or eat them as is. I came up with this recipe after being inspired by something I read in a magazine, and I'm oh, so glad I did! The Dijon mustard here adds a pop of flavor that deepens the experience. I could just eat this right out of the pan (and often do)! But it serves as a wonderful accompaniment to anything on your plate—fish, veggies, or otherwise.

2 to 3 tablespoons (30 to 45 ml) extra virgin olive oil (EVOO)

2 small or 1 large leek, sliced

½ small red onion, chopped small dice

1 pound (450 g) shiitake mushrooms, sliced

½ teaspoon (2 ml) sea salt

½ teaspoon (2 ml) black pepper

1 teaspoon (5 ml) Dijon mustard

1. Heat up the EVOO in a pan over medium heat. Add the leeks and red onions to the pan, and sauté until translucent (about 5 to 10 minutes).

2. Add the mushrooms and sauté for another 5 to 10 minutes or until the mushrooms are tender.

3. Toss with salt and pepper, and then add the Dijon mustard. Toss to combine. Remove from heat.

4. Serve as is or in any creative way imaginable!

LAUREN'S VEGGIE CHILI

SERVES: 6 TO 8

My mom's other specialty growing up was chili. I loved it. In fact, it was one of the three recipes she gave me when I went off to college because it was so easy to make. Chili can be made in huge quantities and can feed a big family or last for many meals. I had to come up with a vegetarian version, and this recipe does the trick! I think it has made my mama proud.

- 2 tablespoons (30 ml) extra virgin olive oil (EVOO)
- 1 large yellow onion, chopped medium dice
- 2 red bell peppers, chopped medium dice
- 2 cloves garlic, minced
- 2 medium zucchinis, chopped medium dice
- 1 pound (450 g) portobello mushrooms, cubed
- 3 medium yams (sweet potatoes), chopped in ½-inch cubes
- 2 tablespoons (30 ml) chili powder
- 1 tablespoon (15 ml) ground cumin

- 1 teaspoon (5 ml) sea salt
- ¼ teaspoon (1 ml) cayenne
- 1 teaspoon (5 ml) dried thyme
- 1 15-ounce (425 g) can diced tomatoes
- 1 15-ounce (425 g) can black beans
- 1 15-ounce (425 g) can white beans
- 1 15-ounce (425 g) can tomato sauce
- 1 to 2 cups (240 to 480 ml) veggie stock (depending on how thick you want the chili)
- 3 cups (200 g) kale or spinach

Optional for garnish: avocado, cilantro, and/or green onions

1. In a heavy soup pot, heat the EVOO on medium heat. Add in the onions and peppers, and sauté until soft (about 10 minutes). Add in the garlic and sauté for another minute.

2. Add in the zucchini, mushrooms, and yams. Toss to combine and cook for another 10 minutes.

3. Add in the spices and toss to combine. Then add the tomatoes, beans, tomato sauce, and veggie stock. Bring to a boil and then reduce to a simmer for about 20 minutes, stirring occasionally.

4. Add in the kale or spinach and cook for another 2 to 3 minutes or until wilted down. Adjust the seasoning.

5. Serve warm. Garnish with avocado, cilantro, and green onions, or anything else you like with your chili.

PESTO-ROASTED TOMATOES

SERVES: 4 TO 6

When I first learned to cook, Ina Garten of the Barefoot Contessa was my inspiration. I bought all of her cookbooks and have easily made over half of the recipes that fill the pages of those books. One of my favorite recipes from her cookbook was the tomatoes roasted with pesto. It was such a simple dish, yet it's so elegant and flavorful. Thankfully, it was easy to make a vegetarian version. All I had to do was swap out the dairy pesto with my vegan one, and voila! Serve these beauties as a side dish to your main attraction, add them to a burger, or even put them on some spaghetti squash "pasta!"

4 to 5 large tomatoes

Drizzle extra virgin olive oil (EVOO)

A pinch of sea salt

A pinch of pepper

A pinch of dried oregano

Pesto (page 149)

Optional: Brazil nut Parmesan "cheese" as topping (page 86)

1. Preheat oven to 425° Fahrenheit (220°C).

2. Cut your tomatoes into ½-inch-thick (1.25 cm) slices, and place them flat on a baking sheet lined with parchment paper.

3. Drizzle them with olive oil, salt, pepper, and oregano (or your spice of choice). Place them in the oven for 10 minutes.

4. After 10 minutes, pull them out and top each tomato slice with about a teaspoon of pesto. At this point, you can sprinkle them with the Brazil nut Parmesan "cheese."

5. Bake the tomatoes for another 7 to 10 minutes, or until the "cheese" starts to brown. Serve as is, or as a side.

GINGER SCALLION VEGGIE BOWL

SERVES: 2 TO 4

When I'm in New York, I make a list and a schedule of restaurants to visit for every meal of the day. One of my favorite restaurants is Peacefood Cafe. And one of my favorite meals from there is the ginger scallion bowl. Since they don't have a Peacefood Cafe in L.A., I had to figure out how to make the bowl myself. Thankfully, I did. Be prepared for this recipe to become one of your new faves.

½ cup (120 ml) extra virgin olive oil (EVOO) or avocado oil

3 tablespoons (45 ml) fresh ginger, minced

6 to 8 scallions, chopped

1 teaspoon (5 ml) kosher salt

1 cup (180 g) quinoa

1 to 2 cups (150 to 300 g) any variation of cooked or roasted veggies that you like (suggest: roasted cauliflower, broccoli, and sweet potatoes)

1 cup sautéed (130 g) kale or Swiss chard

½ cup (75 g) sautéed mushrooms, any variety

1. Heat your oil or avocado oil over medium-high heat until sizzling, but not smoking.

2. Place the minced ginger and chopped scallions in a heatproof bowl (preferably glass).

3. Pour the hot oil over the ginger and scallions.

   Caution: The ginger and scallions will sizzle. Be careful not to burn yourself.

4. Add salt to taste, stir, and let the flavors infuse.

5. Cook the desired amount of quinoa according to the package instructions.

6. To make the bowl, spoon the quinoa into a serving bowl, place your baked/roasted/sautéed veggies on top, and drizzle with the ginger scallion oil.

WALNUT SHIITAKE MUSHROOM TACOS

SERVES: 4

Everyone loves a good taco, right? Growing up, we used to have taco or fajita night once a week during the summer, and I loved it. There was something fun about putting your food together and being able to create your own personalized wrap. My mom used to make teriyaki honey flavored pork to use as the base for our fajitas, and I used to top mine with orange cheddar cheese, tomatoes, lettuce, and sour cream. What you have in the recipe that follows is a vegetarian and vegan-friendly, more-sophisticated version of this old favorite. Bet you can't have just one!

For the walnut shiitake filling:

- 1 pound (450 g) shiitake mushrooms, sautéed in olive oil
- 3 cups (375 g) walnuts
- 1½ (22 ml) tablespoons cumin
- 1 teaspoon (5 ml) ground chili powder
- 2½ (37 ml) tablespoons soy sauce

For the walnut shiitake filling:

1 pound (450 g) shiitake mushrooms, sautéed in olive oil

3 cups (375 g) walnuts

1½ (22 ml) tablespoons cumin

1 teaspoon (5 ml) ground chili powder

2½ (37 ml) tablespoons soy sauce

For the guacamole:

4 avocados

Juice of 1 lime and 1 lemon

1 tablespoon (15 ml) cilantro, chopped

1 minced clove of garlic

Salt and pepper to taste

For the pico de gallo:

4 small tomatoes, diced

2 tablespoons (30 ml) cilantro, roughly chopped

½ onion, small diced

Juice of 1 lime

Sea salt and pepper to taste

For the cashew sour cream:

1 cup (125 g) raw cashews

¼ teaspoon (1 ml) salt

4 tablespoons (60 ml) fresh lemon juice

½ cup (120 ml) water

One bunch of Romaine lettuce or collard greens (to use as taco wraps)

½ cup (50 g) chopped cabbage as topping for the taco

1. To make the shiitake walnut taco filling, pulse together the shiitake mushrooms, walnuts, cumin, chili powder, and soy sauce in a food processor until the walnuts and mushrooms are ground to pea size. Set aside.

2. For the guacamole, mash the avocados in a bowl, and mix in the lime and lemon juice, cilantro, and garlic. Add salt and pepper to taste.

3. For the pico de gallo, mix the diced tomatoes, cilantro, onion, and lime juice. Add salt and pepper to taste, and let it sit for a few minutes to blend all the flavors.

4. For the cashew sour cream, blend the raw cashews, salt, fresh lemon juice, and water in a food processor until smooth. Set aside.

5. To put your taco together, place your walnut shiitake mushroom filling in your lettuce wrap, and top with cashew sour cream, guacamole, pico de gallo, and cabbage.

KITCHARI

SERVES: 6

I've dealt with a lot of gut health issues since I was a kid. (I won't get into the reasons why, but suffice it to say that I was over-medicated and ate mostly processed food and almost no greens.) On the advice of a naturopath, I was told to eat kitchari. Something about the combination of the rice and the mung beans creates a coating in the gut lining to help seal any holes. If you're not into the rice, you can certainly replace it with cauliflower rice. Not sure how to make it? You can actually buy it already prepared in the supermarket. But if you'd rather make your own, simply pulse a head of cauliflower in your food processor until it is the size and look of "rice."

2 tablespoons (30 ml) olive oil

1 onion, chopped small dice

2 tablespoons (30 ml) fresh ginger, minced

1 teaspoon (5 ml) cumin powder

1 head of cauliflower, chopped

1½ (270 g) cups brown basmati rice, uncooked (can replace this with cauliflower rice)

1½ cups (270 g) yellow split peas or mung beans, uncooked

8 to 10 cups water (4¼ liters)

1 teaspoon (5 ml) kosher or Himalayan salt

1½ (7 ml) teaspoons turmeric

1 tablespoon (15 ml) coriander power or seeds

1 bag washed spinach

½ pound (450 g) cherry tomatoes, halved

1. Heat olive oil in a large soup pot over medium heat. Add the onions and sauté for about 5 minutes, until translucent. Add ginger and sauté for a few more minutes, until it starts to brown.

2. Add the cumin and stir, ensuring the ginger is coated.

3. Add the cauliflower and cook until browned. This should take about 5 to 8 minutes. You can turn the heat up to get the browning process going. Just be sure to watch it and stir every few minutes.

4. Add the rice and mung beans. Stir and sauté for about 3 to 5 minutes, just enough to bring out the nuttiness.

5. Add the rest of the spices and about 8 cups of (2 liters) water. Bring the mixture to a boil (lid on). As the mixture starts to reduce and the rice and mung beans absorb the liquid, test the doneness of the beans by tasting them. If they are still hard after most of the liquid has been absorbed, add another cup of water and continue to cook at medium-high heat without a cover. Taste the beans again, and if necessary, add another cup of water and keep cooking. Continue in this fashion until the beans are soft and most of the liquid is absorbed.

6. When almost all of the water is absorbed, add the spinach and tomatoes, and stir. Keep tossing/stirring until the spinach is wilted down.

7. Season with Himalayan salt to taste.

ROASTED BRUSSELS SPROUTS WITH TOASTED PECANS

SERVES: 4

I used to love Thanksgiving and all the fixings when I was growing up, but there was one dish that I stayed far away from: Brussels sprouts. My dad loved them. So my mom would boil some up, and he would happily devour them as I plugged my hose and thanked my lucky stars that Mom didn't make me eat them, too. If you told me then that Brussels sprouts would become one of my favorite veggies, I would have written you off for crazy. But low and behold, thanks to the wonders of caramelization, I now love these green little gems! This recipe is why.

I pound (450 g) Brussels sprouts

1½ to 2 tablespoons (22 to 30 ml) extra virgin olive oil (EVOO)

½ to I teaspoon (7 ml) sea salt

½ teaspoon (2 ml) ground black pepper

¼ cup (30 g) pecans, pieces and halves

Optional: I teaspoon (5 ml) balsamic reduction, store bought or home-made

1. Preheat oven to 375° Fahrenheit (190°C).

2. Cut off the bottoms of the Brussels sprouts and peel some of the leaves off. Place the leaves on an ungreased sheet pan. Cut the remaining sprout in half, and place it on the sheet pan as well. Repeat with the entire pound of Brussels sprouts.

3. Drizzle the sprouts with EVOO, salt, and pepper, and toss with your hands until everything is coated. Bake the sprouts for 10 minutes.

4. At the 10-minute mark, open the oven and sprinkle the sprouts with ¼ cup of pecan pieces and halves (not whole). No tossing necessary—you don't want to disrupt the caramelization process! Bake for another 10 minutes.

5. Pull them out of the oven and drizzle with ½ to I teaspoon (2 to 5 ml) of balsamic reduction if you choose to go this route. Toss to coat. Serve warm.

The leaves will be crispy, just like a good chip, and the cores of the sprouts will be nice and caramelized—so good!!

SPICY OVEN-ROASTED CAULIFLOWER

SERVES: 4

Cauliflower and I have a love-hate relationship. When it's boiled or steamed, we are not friends. But when it's cooked into a pizza crust or roasted and caramelized in the oven, we are best buds. This recipe is a bit spicy, so if you're not into spice, hold off on the red pepper flakes. I promise you it will still be delicious!

1 head cauliflower

2 tablespoons (30 ml) olive oil

½ teaspoon (2 ml) red pepper flakes

Dash of salt and pepper

1. Preheat oven to 375° Fahrenheit (190°C).

2. Cut up cauliflower into bite-size pieces.

3. Place cauliflower pieces on a baking sheet. Drizzle with olive oil, red pepper flakes, salt, and pepper. Toss with your hands to coat all the pieces.

4. Roast in the oven for 25 to 30 minutes. Take it out when it's golden brown on the bottom. Enjoy!

SPICY KALE AND CAULIFLOWER PALEO RICE

SERVES: 4

1 large head of cauliflower, chopped

1 bunch of curly green kale, de-spined, and chopped

2 to 3 tablespoons (30 to 45 ml) sesame oil

2 to 3 tablespoons (30 to 45 ml) extra virgin olive oil (EVOO)

3 cloves garlic, minced

1 handful cilantro, roughly chopped

1 large tomato, chopped small dice

4 tablespoons (60 ml) apple cider vinegar

2 tablespoons (30 ml) coconut aminos

1 teaspoon (5 ml) sea salt

½ teaspoon (2 ml) black pepper

5 scallions, thinly sliced

2 tablespoons (30 ml) siracha sauce

1. Using a food processor, pulse your chopped cauliflower to a rice-like consistency. I find that I have to do this in batches, because if I put too much cauliflower in at one time, not all of it gets "riced." Once all of the cauliflower has been pulsed to "rice," set it aside.

2. Using a food processor (can be the same one—no need to rinse it out), pulse your chopped kale into "rice." Do this is in batches as well, until all of the kale has been "riced." Set aside.

3. Heat up the olive and sesame oil over medium-low heat. Add the cauliflower and kale rice and the rest of the ingredients to the pot, including the siracha. Stir to combine. Turn the heat up to medium-high, and sauté for about 10 to 15 minutes, stirring every 3 to 5 minutes to make sure it doesn't burn.

4. Serve alone, or with some guacamole and/or sweet potato fries.

Basil Oil (page 151)

Spreads, Nut Butters, and Dips

How much do I love thee? Let me count the ways. When I was transitioning from my SAD (Standard American Diet), I started experimenting not only with various types of cooking methods (like roasting), but also with flavor-filled, healthy dips, spreads, butters, and sauces that could help me swallow my healthier food (no pun intended). I could easily have written a cookbook of this chapter alone. But instead, I picked some of my favorites. In here, you will find delicious nut butters and milks you can enjoy for breakfast, a good snack, or anytime of the day. The pestos and infused oils will not only add a layer of flavor to your dishes you never knew existed, but because of their beautiful colors, will also turn them into visual masterpieces (like the beetroot pesto on page 147). So beautiful.

CHOCOLATE HAZELNUT SPREAD

SERVES: 6 TO 8

I used to be so jealous of the kids whose parents let them have Nutella when I was younger. Chocolate that you could spread on bread? Is there anything better? I couldn't think of anything. I still love the taste of Nutella, but the ingredients don't impress me, nor does the stomach ache that follows after I eat it. Since making healthy food taste good is my specialty and passion in life, I assumed I could make a healthier version that I liked just as much. I was right, and the recipe that follows is the proof. You're welcome.

1½ (190 g) cups hazelnuts

½ cup (120 ml) coconut milk (you can also use almond milk)

¼ cup (60 ml) maple syrup

¼ cup (60 ml) unsweetened cocoa powder

1 teaspoon (5 ml) vanilla

Pinch of sea salt

1. Roast the hazelnuts at 350° Fahrenheit (180°C) for 5 to 7 minutes or until barely browned.

2. Let them cool for a few minutes, and then put them in a food processor and blend until smooth (about 3 to 5 minutes, depending on the strength of your food processor).

3. Add the coconut milk, syrup, cocoa powder, vanilla and salt and blend until smooth.

Eat it by the spoonful!

Tip: Scoop out a spoonful of homemade pecan butter (page 141) and top it with some of this chocolate hazelnut spread—it's heaven on a spoon!

ALMOND BUTTER

SERVES: 6 TO 8

I discovered how easy it is to make my own almond butter a few years ago, and honest to goodness, I have not bought a jar in the store since. It's so easy that it just seems wrong not to make it yourself. You literally put nuts in a food processor, press on, and walk away until you get butter. And what's more is that unlike almost all the store-bought versions, there is no added oil of any kind. It's just nuts and whatever spices you add (or don't add). I like to add cinnamon to mine, but you can leave it out or even mess around with any combination of spices as you desire. Use this recipe as your base, and proceed from there.

2 cups (250 g) raw almonds

1½ teaspoon (7 ml) cinnamon

¼ teaspoon (1 ml) sea salt

1. Place the almonds on a sheet pan in an even layer and bake at 350° Fahrenheit (180°C) for 5 minutes.

2. Let the roasted almonds cool for 5 minutes, and then place them in a food processor along with the cinnamon and sea salt. Blend them for about 2 to 5 minutes until your "butter" forms!

3. Place in a jar with an airtight lid, and keep in the fridge for up to three weeks. (It won't last that long—it'll be gone in a few days!)

PECAN BUTTER

SERVES: 6 TO 8

I like to call this crack butter. The first time I made this for my husband, he didn't believe me when I told him there was no sugar in it. The pecans are naturally sweet, and they have such a unique flavor that it tastes like there are at least 5 other ingredients in this (including sugar). Cinnamon plays a key role in this recipe when I make it. If you don't like cinnamon, feel free to leave it out.

3 cups (375 g) pecans, whole or pieces are both fine

1½ (7 ml) teaspoon cinnamon

¼ (1 ml) teaspoon sea salt

1. Place the pecans on a sheet pan in an even layer and bake at 350° Fahrenheit (180°C) for 5 minutes.

   Warning: *Pecans burn easily! If you have a hot oven, reduce the temperature to 325° Fahrenheit (160°C), and check the pecans at 2 to 3 minutes. Be careful!*

2. Let the roasted pecans cool for 5 minutes, and then place them in a food processor along with the cinnamon and sea salt. Blend for about 2 to 5 minutes until your "butter" forms!

3. Place in a jar with an airtight lid, and keep in the fridge for up to three weeks. (It won't last that long—it'll be gone in a few days!)

ALMOND PECAN BUTTER

SERVES: 6 TO 8

Ok, now we're just getting fancy. As you can see, once you have a base for nut butter, and once you understand the differences in the nuts (i.e., almonds take longer to turn into butter because they are heavier than pecans), you can start messing around with your own nut butter combinations. I love mixing almonds and pecans together because, quite frankly, they are my two favorite nuts next to macadamias.

2 cups (250 g) raw almonds

1 cup (125 g) pecans

1½ (7 ml) teaspoons cinnamon

¼ (1 ml) teaspoon sea salt

1. Place the nuts on a sheet pan in an even layer. Bake at 350° Fahrenheit (180°C) for 5 minutes.

2. Let the nuts cool for 5 minutes, and then place them in a food processor along with the cinnamon and sea salt. Blend until smooth. You may have to scrape the sides along the way.

3. Place in a jar with an airtight lid, and keep in the fridge for up to three weeks. (It won't last that long—it'll be gone in a few days!)

SPIRULINA PESTO

SERVES: 4 TO 6

When I went to Rootz Cafe in Steamboat Springs, CO, I fell in love with their spirulina pesto! It was served over a bowl of broccolini and two over-easy eggs. It was heaven in my mouth. The chef was gracious enough to give me the recipe! I've made a few tweaks, but here it is.

¼ cup (30 g) pine nuts

10 cloves garlic, peeled and roughly chopped

1 handful fresh cilantro

1 handful fresh basil

1½ teaspoon (7 ml) spirulina powder

1 teaspoon (5 ml) sea salt

½ teaspoon (2 ml) ground black

4 tablespoons (60 ml) fresh lemon juice

½ cup (120 ml) extra virgin olive oil (EVOO)

1. Pulse the nuts and garlic in a food processor into a paste.

2. Add the cilantro, basil, spirulina, salt, pepper, and lemon juice. Turn on the food processor, and as it's running, pour the EVOO into it. Add more if the pesto is too thick.

3. Serve this over pasta, spaghetti squash, on pizza, or anything else where you might use pesto!

BEET SUNFLOWER SEED PESTO

SERVES: 4 TO 6

One of my favorite restaurants in Denver is Root Down. I had one of the most glorious meals there a few years back: an arugula salad with hazelnuts, basil oil, and this beetroot pesto. The salad itself was beautiful—a true sight for the eyes—and the flavors did not disappoint. I recipe-tested my own version of this radiant pesto when I got home and came up with this recipe. It's a home run!

10 cloves of garlic, roughly chopped

¼ cup (30 g) sunflower seeds, roasted

¼ cups (30 g) pine nuts, roasted

4 tablespoons (60 ml) fresh lemon juice

1 handful of fresh basil

1 handful of fresh cilantro

3 small to medium-size red or golden beets, cooked

1 teaspoon (5 ml) sea salt

½ teaspoon (2 ml) black pepper

1 cup (175 ml) extra virgin olive oil (EVOO)

1. Cook the beets anyway you like—bake or boil them whole, or buy them pre-cooked.

2. Blend everything except for the EVOO together in a food processor. While the processor is running, slowly add 1 cup of EVOO, and let it combine. If you find the pesto is too thick, add some more lemon juice or EVOO. Just be sure to taste as you go.

That's it! You can store this in the fridge in an airtight container with plastic wrap directly touching the top of the pesto for up to two days. Otherwise, store it in the freezer for up to three months. It's great to have on hand for those days when you need a gourmet meal in a pinch!

BASIC VEGAN PESTO

SERVES: 4 TO 6

I always, always (like always) have at least one—usually two—jars of pesto in my freezer. It's such an amazing sauce to pull out in a pinch whenever I need to put a meal together in no time. Before you go to work in the morning, pull out the jar from the freezer and put it in the fridge. When you get home at night, you can pop a spaghetti squash in the oven and toss it with pesto for a quick meal. Add some greens and some pine nuts or walnuts to make it a bit heartier, and you've got a dinner for the whole family to enjoy. You can also use this pesto in any number of dishes—including the pesto-roasted tomatoes (page 123) and the chickpea soup with pesto (page 79). Set yourself up for success: make sure you keep this on hand!

¼ cup (30 g) walnuts

¼ cup (30 g) pine nuts

7 to 8 cloves of garlic, whole

1½ teaspoons (7 ml) kosher salt

1 teaspoon (5 ml) pepper

4 oz (4 cups/100 g) fresh basil leaves

1 to 1½ cups (175 to 295 ml) extra virgin olive oil (depending on how you like it)

1. Pulse the nuts, garlic, salt, and pepper in a food processor for about 30 seconds (until a paste forms).

2. Add in your basil leaves and turn on the food processor again. Slowly add in the oil as the processor is running.

3. Store in jars (freezes well). Keep plenty on hand for any number of dishes.

> *Variations: You can use any variation of nuts and seeds you like. It can be all seeds, all nuts, or a mixture of the two. As long as it adds up to a ½ cup, you're golden! My favorite nuts to use are walnuts or pine nuts My favorite seeds are pumpkin or sunflower.*

BASIL OIL

SERVES: 4 TO 6

This is one of those beautiful finishing touches that can take a dish and make it elegant in a flash! I use this in the arugula salad recipe (page 74), but you can use this any way you'd like. Drizzle some on any salad to add an extra layer; drizzle it over any main dish; or use it in place of (or in addition to) hot sauce on your scrambled eggs or frittata! When it comes to basil, garlic, and oil, you really can't go wrong.

2 cups (50 g) fresh basil leaves

⅔ cup (150 ml) extra virgin olive oil (EVOO)

2 garlic cloves, minced

Salt and pepper, to taste

1. Blend everything together in a food processor or blender until smooth.

2. Store in an airtight container in the fridge until ready to use!

DIJON MAPLE DRESSING

SERVES: 4

Everybody loves a good salad dressing, and it seems that—just like guacamole—everyone has a go-to. This is mine. Admittedly, when it's just my husband and I at home, I tend to just dress my salads with a good balsamic vinegar (read: from Italy) and some EVOO. But when guests are coming over (or when I'm starting to get bored), I throw this into the mix. The maple syrup adds a hint of sweet that just slightly turns up the volume on the taste, and the Dijon adds that fifth flavor of umami to the party.

1 tablespoon (15 ml) Dijon mustard

1 tablespoon (15 ml) maple syrup

3 tablespoons (45 ml) balsamic (Substitute red wine vinegar if you want to change it up.)

6 tablespoons (90 ml) extra virgin olive oil (EVOO) – Up it to 8 tablespoons if you want to.

1 clove garlic, minced

Lots of pepper (about ½ teaspoon/2 ml)

Pinch of sea salt (about ⅛ teaspoon/0.5 ml)

1. Put all the ingredients in a jar with a lid and shake, making sure everything is incorporated.

2. Pour over any salad of your choice and toss. Enjoy!

THE ACCIDENTAL PALEO

Almond Butter Banana Cashew Cheesecake
(page 158)

Desserts

As a former pastry chef and a sugar addict since birth, dessert is in my blood. I don't want to imagine a world where dessert doesn't exist. That said, I much prefer to get my dessert without a side of guilt and without the harmful effects of processed sugar. Thankfully, over the last eight years, I have spent too many hours in the kitchen to count, testing recipes that could pass my sugar-addicted palate. What I've come up with is a collection of healthy desserts that can keep any sweet tooth in check.

RAW BANANA BLUEBERRY STRAWBERRY CASHEW CHEESECAKE

SERVES: 12

I love cheesecake. But unfortunately, cheesecake doesn't love me. It's a shame, too. Because I learned how to make the most creamy, most delicious cheesecake from a master pastry chef while working at a fancy restaurant in Vancouver many years ago. Oh well—onward and upward! His recipe served as inspiration for me to make a vegan alternative, and I think that you will find that I have succeeded! This recipe is creamy, smooth and packed full of flavor. It uses the natural sweetness of the berries and banana rather than any kind of processed sugar, which is a huge bonus! Turns out you can have your cake and eat it too. You're welcome!

Crust:

1 cup (125 g) hazelnuts	8 large dates, pitted
1 cup (75 g) coconut flakes	⅛ teaspoon (0.5 ml) sea salt
1 tablespoon (15 ml) vanilla	

Banana blueberry filling:

3 ripe bananas	2 teaspoons (10 ml) chia seeds
1 13.5oz (390 g) can coconut milk (full-fat)	½ cup (100 g) coconut manna
	1½ cups (190 g) raw cashews, soaked
1 cup (100 g) fresh blueberries	2 teaspoons (10 ml) vanilla

Strawberry topping:

1 package frozen strawberries or 2 cups (400 g) fresh

2 teaspoons (10 ml) chia seeds

1. Blend all the crust ingredients together in a food processor for about a minute or until finely ground. Pour the crust into the bottom of a spring form pan and pat down evenly and firmly. Set aside.

2. Blend the banana blueberry ingredients in a high-powered blender until smooth (about 1 minute). Pour over the crust in the pan. Place in the freezer to set for at least 4 hours (or overnight).

3. When the filling is mostly set, make your strawberry topping. If using frozen strawberries, heat them up in a pot with a splash of water until they are thawed. Then place them in a blender with 2 teaspoons (10 ml) of chia seeds.

4. When ready to serve, pull the cake out of the freezer and put it into the fridge. The strawberry filling will melt a little bit down the side of the cake. Place a whole strawberry in the middle of the top of the cake for garnish.

ALMOND BUTTER BANANA CASHEW CHEESECAKE

SERVES: 12

I was so excited about the success of my banana blueberry strawberry vegan cheese-cake that I decided I needed to play around with it some more. I love almond butter and banana together, so I figured, why not make it a dessert? And why not make it a cheesecake? That is exactly what I did with this recipe. Expect another smooth, creamy, dairy-free cheesecake you can feel good about eating and feeding to your family and friends.

For the crust:

¼ cups (30 g) Brazil nuts

¾ cups (95 g) raw almonds

1 cup (75 g) unsweetened coconut flakes

1 tablespoon (15 ml) cacao nibs

2 tablespoons (30 ml) vanilla

8 large dates, pitted

⅛ teaspoon (0.5 ml) sea salt

For the banana filling:

3 ripe bananas

1 13.5-fl oz. can (390 g) coconut milk

2 teaspoons (10 ml) chia seeds

⅓ cup (75 g) coconut manna

1½ (190 g) cups cashews, soaked overnight

2 teaspoons (10 ml) vanilla

For the almond butter topping:

1 cup (266 g) almond butter

1 teaspoon (5 ml) coconut oil

2 teaspoons (10 ml) chia seeds

Optional: **Melted dark chocolate and crushed almonds as topping**

1. To make the crust, place all the ingredients in a food processor and blend for about 30 to 60 seconds. When you pick up a handful of crust in your hands and form a fist, a ball of crust should remain intact. That's how you know it is wet enough. If the ball of crust doesn't remain intact, add another date and process it again.

2. Dump the crust onto the bottom of a springform pan. Pack and pat the crust down into an even layer along the bottom of the pan. Set aside.

3. To make the banana filling, place all ingredients in a high-powered blender and blend on high speed until smooth (about a minute). Pour the filling over top of the crust, ensuring it's evenly spread.

4. Place the cake in the freezer to set for at least 4 hours.

5. When the cake is set, make the almond butter filling. Over medium-low heat, melt together the coconut oil, almond butter and chia seeds. Stir with a spatula until smooth and combined.

6. Remove the cake from the freezer, and pour the almond butter filling on top in an even layer, using a spatula to ensure the filling is evenly spread all the way to the edges.

7. Place the cake back in the freezer to set for another few hours. Once it is set, you can place the cake in the fridge and store it there until it's ready to serve.

8. Serve as is. Or, if you want to get fancy, you can serve it with a drizzle of melted dark chocolate and/or a sprinkling of crushed almonds. Enjoy!

Note: This recipe calls for soaked cashews for the banana filling. For best results, soak them overnight.

VEGAN PUMPKIN CHEESECAKE CHIA SEED PUDDING

SERVES 6 TO 10

I used to hate pumpkin pie when I was growing up. I really wanted to like it, but for some reason, I just couldn't get down with the flavor. Now I'm utterly obsessed with pumpkin in all forms: roasted with some EVOO, pureed in my pie, and—thanks to this recipe—congealed with chia seeds in a pudding. Serve up this pudding for your dairy-free guests around the holidays, and they'll never miss the pumpkin pie!

1 cup canned pumpkin puree

2 tablespoons (30 ml) chia seeds soaked in 4 tablespoons (60 ml) water for 10 minutes, until gelatinous

½ cup (120 ml) coconut cream

1 cup (240 ml) unsweetened almond milk

⅓ cup (60 g) dates, pitted

Pinch of kosher salt

1 tablespoon (15 ml) ground cinnamon

½ teaspoon (2 ml) ground ginger

½ teaspoon (2 ml) nutmeg

⅛ teaspoon (0.5 ml) ground cloves

1 tablespoon (15 ml) maple syrup

1 teaspoon (5 ml) vanilla

1. Blend together all ingredients in a food processor or blender, chill, and enjoy!

2. Keeps in the fridge for three to five days.

SALTED DARK CHOCOLATE GOJI BERRY ALMOND BARK

SERVES: 4 TO 6

This is one of those recipes that makes you want to pat yourself on the back when you're done. Why? Because it only has 4 ingredients, is easy to make, tastes absolutely delicious (with hardly any sugar), and looks like an elegant masterpiece. I love serving this up around the holidays because of the beautiful redness of the goji berries. And it makes for a lovely hostess gift if you're going to a party and want to bring something original and delicious. The darker the chocolate you use, the less sugar you have to contend with. I recommend 85% dark chocolate from Green & Black's because it's smooth and creamy without being too bitter, but feel free to use whatever chocolate you like best.

2 3.5-ounce (200 g) bars plus 2 small pieces 85% dark chocolate (I prefer Green & Black's Organics)

I handful goji berries

I handful whole roasted raw almonds

Pinch of Celtic sea salt or Himalayan pink salt

1. If your almonds haven't already been roasted, roast them at 350° Fahrenheit (180°C) for five minutes. Set aside to cool.

2. Break up your two chocolate bars into a double boiler. Stir until the chocolate is completely melted. Remove from the heat.

3. In order to temper the chocolate, add your two extra pieces of dark chocolate to the bowl of melted chocolate and stir until melted.

4. Poor the chocolate onto a parchment- or silicone mat-covered sheet pan. Using a spatula, spread the chocolate into somewhat of a rectangular shape, ensuring the chocolate is about ⅛ to ¼-inch (0.6 cm) thick.

5. Sprinkle with as many goji berries and almonds as your heart desires! Then finish it off with a pinch of Celtic sea salt (or Himalayan pink salt).

6. Let it set in the fridge. Once it's completely set (cooled), break it into bite-sized pieces. Store in the fridge for up to two weeks.

> *Note: This recipe calls for melting chocolate in a double boiler (step 2). To make a double boiler, heat up about an inch of water in a pot. When it comes to a boil, turn off the heat and place a metal bowl over top of the pot so that it rests there.*

VEGAN "COOKIES AND CREAM" MILKSHAKE

SERVES: 1

I am a huge fan of the vegan restaurant Cafe Gratitude here in L.A., but I live a gazillion miles away from it. (Okay, not that far, but it's at least an hour's drive.) One of my favorite cheat meals when I go there is their chocolate almond buttercup shake. Since I don't always feel like driving an hour for a milkshake that's not-so-good for me (not to mention the hefty, though worthy price tag), I had to come up with my own version. This recipe is more like the cookies and cream version of the Cafe Gratitude one, and it's easily 75 percent less sweet. That's music to my ears, and I hope it will be to yours too.

3 scoops vegan vanilla ice cream
(store-bought or your favorite homemade kind)

1 tablespoon (15 ml) cacao nibs

1 tablespoon (15 ml) almond butter
(preferably homemade)

1 cup (240 ml) coconut or almond milk

Blend on high until smooth. Enjoy!

VEGAN CHOCOLATE ALMOND SHAKE

SERVES: 1

Another one of my favorite restaurants in L.A. is called Juicy Ladies. They serve up healthy organic meals, and on a hot summer's day, my favorite Juicy Ladies treat is their chocolate almond shake. But like Cafe Gratitude, Juicy Ladies is pretty far away from me (more like a million miles rather than a gazillion), so I had to figure out how to make their shake on my own. This recipe comes so close to the original that I'm pretty sure it can be considered the approved doppelganger. I let my taste buds do the investigating, and I think you'll love what I've come up with.

1 to 2 large dates, chopped

1 tablespoon (15 ml) cocoa nibs

1 teaspoon (5 ml) vanilla powder

1 teaspoon (5 ml) cocoa powder

2 tablespoons (30 ml) almond butter

½ cup (120 ml) coconut water

2 cups (280 g) ice

Place all ingredients in a Vitamix or blender and blend until smooth. Enjoy!

ALMOND BUTTER CUPS

MAKES 8 TO 12 CUPS

This is another one of those recipes that makes me incredibly happy because first of all, it makes me feel like I'm eating dessert. Second of all, I am. But third of all, these have no added sugar besides whatever sugar is in the chocolate you use. Oh, and it only has two ingredients! Feel free to use any nut butter you'd like, and be prepared to enjoy a delicious treat without a side of guilt.

1 bar (100 g) dark chocolate (I prefer Green & Black's 85%, but you can use whatever you want.)

1 cup (266 g) homemade almond or pecan butter
(see recipes on pages 140 and 141)
or your favorite store-bought nut butter

1. Line a Pyrex dish or plate with 6 or 7 silicone cupcake liners. If you only have paper liners, that's fine too. Set aside.

2. Melt your chocolate bar by breaking it up into small pieces and heating it over a double boiler. (See page 163 for instructions on how to make a double boiler.) You can also use a microwave, if you prefer.

3. Once the chocolate is melted, spoon out about a teaspoon of chocolate and place it in the cupcake liner, pushing some of the chocolate up along the sides of the liner as you go (should come about ½ way up the liner). Make sure that the bottom of the cup is completely covered in chocolate, though it doesn't have to be a thick coating. Repeat with the rest of your liners.

4. Place the chocolate shells in the fridge to set, which shouldn't take more than 10 minutes.

5. Once the chocolate has set, spoon about a tablespoon of pecan butter into each shell and smooth out so it's flat. The butter should come just below the top of the chocolate shell.

6. Using your remaining melted chocolate, spoon out a teaspoon and smooth it out over the pecan butter using the back of your spoon, creating a seal to the shell. You have to work fast, though, because the pecan butter is cold and the chocolate is hot!

7. Place the cups in the refrigerator to set, and then enjoy to your heart's content!

8. The cups should last for at least 2 weeks in the fridge, if not longer. Enjoy!

CASSANDRA'S GLUTEN-FREE COCONUT BANANA CHOCOLATE CHIP MUFFINS

MAKES 12 TO 15 MUFFINS

My friend Cassandra (the one who got me into cooking and who still loves me even though I made her eat a boxed cake once) is an all-around amazing chef. She and her husband opened up a string of juice shops called Clover Juice here in L.A. a few years ago, but that doesn't stop her from rolling up her sleeves and baking from time to time. She had me over for muffins and tea when her son was a few months old (and I was pregnant and craving everything under the sun), and she served up these muffins right out of the oven. She served them with a side of coconut oil, which we smeared onto each bite and watched it melt into the steam. So. Yum. She was gracious enough to share the recipe with me, and after making a few tweaks, I'm now sharing it with you. Enjoy your new favorite muffin recipe! And thanks, Cassandra!

- 1¾ cup (415 ml) Bob's Red Mills Paleo Flour
- ¼ cup (60 ml) almond meal (you can substitute with chia or flax meal)
- 1 teaspoon (5 ml) cinnamon
- 1 teaspoon (5 ml) baking soda
- 1 teaspoon (5 ml) guar gum
- ½ teaspoon (2 ml) sea salt
- ¼ cup (60 ml) coconut sugar
- ¼ cup (60 ml) coconut cream

- ¼ cup (60 ml) non-dairy milk
- ¼ cup (60 ml) coconut oil (melted)
- 2 bananas, smashed
- 2 eggs (can substitute with 2 flax eggs to make it vegan)
- 1 teaspoon (5 ml) vanilla
- 1 to 2 tablespoons (15 to 30 ml) pure maple syrup
- ½ cup vegan (90 g) chocolate chips
- ½ cup (40 g) coconut flakes (or shredded)

1. Preheat oven to 350° Fahrenheit (180°C).

2. Combine liquid ingredients in a bowl. Set aside.

3. In a larger bowl, combine all dry ingredients except for chocolate chips and coconut flakes. Pour the liquid ingredients over the dry ones. Toss until just combined (you don't want to over stir these). Add in the chocolate chips and coconut flakes.

4. Scoop the dough with an ice cream scoop into cupcake liners or silicone cupcake liners. (Makes about 12 to 14, depending on the size of the scoop.) Bake for 10 minutes, rotate, and bake another 10 minutes or until a toothpick poked into the muffin comes out dry.

COCONUT WHIPPED CREAM WITH BERRIES

SERVES: 4

This is another one of those super easy, beautifully elegant, healthy desserts that is a sure crowd pleaser. Because it's so easy to make, it's the perfect dessert to make when you are limited in time and have guests coming over for brunch, lunch, or dinner (or hungry children beating down the door for a dessert or snack). Just remember to chill the coconut milk the night before. Better yet, do what I do: always keep a can of coconut milk in the fridge so you can pull it out as needed. Serve up this recipe with the freshest organic berries you can find. You might also consider adding this as a topping for any of the pudding recipes in this book, or anything you would normally put whipped cream on.

1 13.5-ounce can (400 ml) coconut milk, full-fat, refrigerated overnight

¼ (1 ml) teaspoon vanilla

¼ (1 ml) teaspoon real maple syrup

Fresh organic berries

1. Separate the solid coconut milk from the liquid (this happens naturally in the fridge), and place the solid part in a bowl fitted with a whisk attachment.

2. Add the vanilla and maple syrup. Whip until smooth and creamy!

3. To make your bowl, place your favorite berries in a bowl and top with the coconut whipped cream!

ALMOND MEAL POWER BITES

MAKES 24

As a sugar addict, I have an Achilles heel when it comes to dessert. Cookies are part of that. I challenged myself to come up with a cookie recipe with a good texture that would satisfy my sweet tooth without undoing me. This recipe does the trick! They are so good for you, you can even consider eating them as a post-workout snack for breakfast in the morning!

3 large bananas, mashed

¼ cup (60 g) almond butter (preferably homemade—page 140)

¼ cup (60 g) peanut butter (can sub almond butter if you prefer)

1 teaspoon (5 ml) vanilla

1 tablespoon (15 ml) coconut oil, melted

3 cups (100 g) fresh almond meal (I use the meal leftover from making almond milk. If using dried almond meal, use 2 cups instead.)

¼ cup (30 g) flax seed meal

1 teaspoon (5 ml) baking powder

¼ teaspoon (1 ml) sea salt

1 tablespoon (15 ml) cinnamon

½ cup (45 g) vegan chocolate chips

1. Preheat oven to 350° Fahrenheit (180°C).

2. Mash the bananas in a bowl with a fork. Add the rest of the ingredients to the bowl, including the chocolate chips. Stir to combine.

3. Using a tablespoon, scoop out a tablespoon-size ball of cookie dough, and place it on a parchment paper-lined cookie sheet. Squish down the cookie slightly with your fingers. Continue this with the rest of your cookie dough, leaving only about an inch between the cookies (they don't spread during baking).

4. Bake for 8 minutes. Then rotate them, and bake for another 5 minutes or until browned.

5. Store cookies in the refrigerator for up to five days.

CHOCOLATE CHIA SEED PUDDING

Ch-Ch-Ch-Chia! I still can't believe I'm using the very same chia seeds to cook and bake with that I used to watch on TV growing up in the 80's! But low and behold, chia seeds have stood the test of time. And with good reason! When it comes to baking and cooking without eggs, you need something that will gelatinize the way an egg does. Chia seeds do just that by sucking up the moisture and congealing to bring everything together. In this recipe, the chia seeds are the binder, but the chocolate is the main attraction. Say goodbye to your store-bought too-many-ingredient pudding, and say hello to your new friend.

2 to 3 dates, pitted

1¾ cup (415 ml) coconut milk, full-fat

¼ cup (60 ml) almond milk (or other nut milk)

2 tablespoons (30 ml) cocoa powder

1 teaspoon (5 ml) vanilla

¼ cup (30 g) cashews (optional)

½ teaspoon (2 ml) sea salt

1 teaspoon (5 ml) cinnamon

1½ tablespoon (22 ml) real maple syrup

½ cup (86 g) black chia seeds

Optional: sliced bananas, slivered almonds, vegan chocolate chips as possible toppings

1. Place everything in a blender except for the chia seeds. Blend until smooth (about 1 to 2 minutes).

2. Add the chia seeds in and blend for another 30 seconds or until smooth.

3. Pour the pudding into a dish or into individual containers, and let set in the fridge for 1 to 2 hours. Serve plain, or with sliced bananas, slivered almonds, vegan chocolate chips, o0r whatever your heart desires!

DARK CHOCOLATE RASPBERRY BARS

SERVES: 12

These are kind of the bomb dot com. I'm just saying. Like the chocolate goji berry almond bark, these have a beautiful color to them, so they are a perfect treat to serve up around the holidays. They also happen to be incredibly delicious with a wonderful texture: crunchy and chewy without being too sweet. Aside from the raspberries (natural sugar) and the dark chocolate, there is no added sugar. Yet another guilt-free dessert for you to add to your repertoire!

1 cup (125 g) frozen raspberries

1 teaspoon (5 ml) arrowroot starch

Coconut oil for greasing the pan

¾ cup (96 g) coconut flour

½ cup (40 g) coconut flakes

½ teaspoon (2 ml) baking soda

¼ teaspoon (1 ml) sea salt

½ cup (120 ml) coconut oil at room temp (solid)

½ cup (75 g) coconut sugar

1 cup (150 g) pumpkin seeds, roughly chopped

6 to 8 ounces (170 to 225 g) 85% organic dark chocolate (my favorite is Green & Blacks Organics), roughly broken up

1. Preheat the oven to 350° Fahrenheit (180°C). Mix the raspberries and the arrowroot starch together in a bowl and set aside.

2. Grease an 8x8-inch square (20x20 cm) pan with coconut oil, and line the bottom with parchment paper. Set aside.

3. In a large bowl, mix the coconut flour, coconut flakes, baking soda, sea salt, coconut oil, coconut sugar, and chopped pumpkin seeds together until crumbly but sticky enough that if you make a ball with it, it sticks together.

4. Set 1 cup of the mixture aside. Place the rest of the mixture evenly along the bottom of your prepared pan. This is your crust, so make sure it's ¼- to ½-inch (0.6 to 1.25 cm) thick at least. Pat it down as you smooth it out. Bake it for 10 minutes or until brown.

5. When it comes out of the oven, sprinkle the chocolate liberally all over the crust (it won't cover it completely, but make it as even as possible). Then cover the chocolate with your raspberries. Finally, sprinkle the leftover cup of your crumble mixture on top of the raspberries.

6. Place the pan back in the oven and bake for 25 to 30 minutes, rotating it half way through, until the tops of the squares are browned.

7. Let cool, cut into squares, and store in the fridge for up to one week or in the freezer for up to three months!

CHOCOLATE BANANA PUDDING

SERVES: 4 TO 6

Is there a better pair than chocolate and banana? Ok, maybe chocolate and peanut butter, but since that's not a paleo-approved treat, chocolate and bananas it is! I'm so glad I got over my skepticism when it came to using avocados in sweet dishes, because they really do make you feel like you're eating a dairy-filled creamy pudding. They are quite the wonder fruit, wouldn't you say? This recipe for chocolate banana pudding is rich, silky, and smooth. Not too sweet, but just sweet enough. It's a perfect mom-approved, kid-tested recipe if you're looking for something nutritious for your family.

2 ripe avocados

1 large or 2 medium ripe bananas

5 tablespoons (75 ml) unsweetened cocoa powder

3 small dates

1 teaspoon (5 ml) vanilla extract

1 teaspoon (5 ml) ground cinnamon

1 tablespoon (15 ml) maple syrup (or honey or agave)

3 tablespoons (45 ml) almond or coconut milk

Pinch of salt

1. Place all ingredients in a food processor or blender and blend until smooth. Do a taste test for sweetness. If you want it a bit sweeter, add in another ½ teaspoon (2 ml) of maple syrup at a time, blend, and taste again.

2. Chill the pudding in the refrigerator either in individual jars or one big bowl. Serve with fresh fruit (I like bananas or strawberries), vegan chocolate chips, crushed nuts, or anything you want!

Golden Milk (page 186)

Drinks

I love eating. Like, a lot. But sometimes, thirst manifests itself as hunger. And sometimes, all you really need is a big tall glass of water. But sometimes, I like something a little stronger than water, something that fools my taste buds into thinking that I'm eating a decadent afternoon treat. These recipes range from infused tea to heavy eggnog, and each one can serve a purpose depending on the occasion, and depending on your reason for reaching for something liquid. Enjoy the Vegan Eggnog (page 192) around the holidays, and treat yourself to a refreshing **Ginger Mint Iced Tea** (page 197) on the next hot summer's day.

VANILLA ALMOND MILK CHAI LATTE

SERVES 1

I posted this recipe on YouTube a few years ago and it got over 32,000 views and counting! And with good reason—it's amazing. I love having vegan lattes to satisfy my craving for sweets, mostly because they last longer. (I usually hoover down a dessert, but a hot tea is too warm for me to consume in such a short period of time.) This recipe is easy to make, and incredibly delicious. Enjoy!

For the chai latte mix:

- 1 tablespoon (25 ml) ground cinnamon
- 1½ teaspoons (7 ml) nutmeg
- 1 teaspoon (5 ml) ground cloves
- 3 tablespoons (45 ml) vanilla powder

For the rest:

- 1 chai tea bag
- 1½ (360 ml) cups boiling water
- 1 cup (240 ml) almond milk

1. Mix together the spices and vanilla powder. Set aside.

2. Boil your water, and pour it into a tall mug. Steep the chai tea bag in it for as long as you like (about 1 to 4 minutes, depending on how strong you like it).

3. While the tea steeps, froth your almond milk. If you don't have a milk frother, just heat up the almond milk in a saucepan until warm.

4. Take the tea bag out of your mug and add ½ to 1 teaspoon of your spice mix and stir until combined. Then add your almond milk. Sprinkle with ground cinnamon, and sweeten if you like, and enjoy!

Tip: You can store the rest of your mix in an airtight container at room temperature for as long as you like.

GOLDEN MILK

SERVES 4 TO 6

I feel like golden milk is all the rage these days, and with good reason. Ginger is wonderful for digestion, and turmeric is great for inflammation. The coconut milk makes for some good fat, and the cinnamon adds a hint of flavor and another layer of nutrition! Enjoy this recipe warm, or stick it in the fridge and enjoy it cold as well!

4 cups (960 ml) filtered water

3-inch (8 cm) piece of fresh turmeric, peeled and sliced

3-inch (8 cm) piece of fresh ginger, peeled and sliced

2 cans coconut milk, full-fat

2 cinnamon sticks

1 teaspoon (5 ml) coconut oil

1. Bring 4 cups of water to a boil, and then place the ginger and turmeric in the pot. Turn the heat down and let it simmer gently for 20 minutes.

2. Add the coconut milk and cinnamon sticks to the pot, and let that simmer gently for another 20 minutes.

3. Lastly, stir in the coconut oil until it melts. Serve warm with a sprinkle of cinnamon. You can also drink it cold! Golden milk stores in the fridge for up to 4 days.

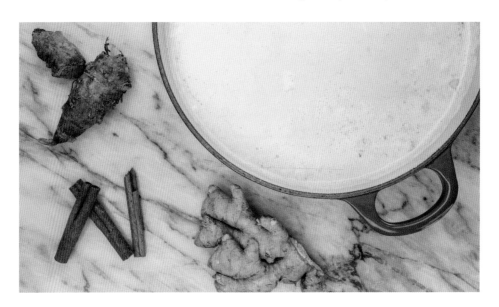

COCONUT MILK

SERVES: 8 TO 10

We drink a lot of nut milk in our house, and when I realized how much coconut milk specifically we were drinking (and didn't love the ingredient list on the store-bought label), I decided there must be a way to make this myself. What I found was easier than I could have ever imagined. This recipe is the most basic coconut milk possible, as it uses shredded coconut and water rather than coconut meat. I'm sure using coconut meat would yield a richer flavor, but honestly, this recipe tastes so velvety and delicious that I haven't even bothered trying to make it any other way. Add it to your grainless granola for a midday snack, use it in your protein shakes, or dress it up with some cinnamon and nutmeg for a festive drink!

I cup (240 ml) organic shredded coconut milk
2 cups (475 ml) filtered water, boiled

1. Place coconut and boiled water in a high-powered blender. Blend on high speed until smooth (about 1 minute).

2. Place a cheesecloth over a metal or glass bowl, and pour the coconut milk over the cheesecloth. Once it's cool enough to handle, wring out the coconut milk through the cheesecloth, squeezing and twisting until all you have left in the cloth is coconut pulp.

3. Save the pulp for smoothies or baking (or discard). Pour the coconut milk into a glass jar, and store in the fridge for two to three days.

HAZELNUT ALMOND MILK

SERVES 6 TO 10

I am kind of obsessed with this food blogger in Toronto named Angela Liddon of *Oh She Glows*. She has a recipe for hazelnut almond milk that I've adapted here, and I have to say: I like it better than plain almond milk. The hazelnuts are a bit heavier, and they add a layer of richness that almonds alone do not have. Be mindful, though. Hazelnuts can be bitter. While I usually leave out dates when making almond milk, when I tried doing that in this recipe, I didn't love the taste. So, do keep that date in there to cut the bitterness. The original recipe actually calls for three, so we're already ahead!

¾ cup (95 g) raw almonds, soaked at least 6 hours

¼ cup (30 g) hazelnuts, soaked at least 6 hours

5 cups (1¼ liters) water

1 teaspoon (5 ml) vanilla

½ teaspoon (2 ml) cinnamon

1 date

1. Soak the nuts overnight in water. If you are impatient, and don't want to wait all night, just be sure to soak them for at least 6 hours.

2. Strain the nuts and place them in a blender with water. Blend until smooth.

3. Pour the mixture through a cheesecloth into a bowl to remove any impurities. (You can buy the cheesecloth in the baking section of any grocery store.) I also put a colander under the cheesecloth, to ensure I don't get any impurities in the finished product! Repeat the process with the second batch of almonds and hazelnuts. Then, ring out the cheesecloth, trapping the nut meal in the cloth, and let the remaining "milk" drain into the bowl.

4. Pour the purified hazelnut almond milk back in the blender or food processor. Add in the vanilla and cinnamon, and blend. Enjoy!

> *Note: This recipe calls for soaked almonds and hazelnuts. For best results, soak them overnight. And if not overnight, be sure to soak them at least 6 hours.*

PROTEINS AND GREENS SHAKE

SERVES 1

I was drinking a particular brand of protein powder in my shakes for the longest time, but when I discovered I might have an intolerance to flax, I had to stop using it. I soon discovered that almost all vegan protein powders have flax in them, and the ones that don't, simply didn't taste good to me. As a working mama who often doesn't have time to do more than make a shake in the morning, I needed a fix, and fast! Thankfully, I recently found a protein powder from Arbonne that has no flavor and no flax, and I have been using it in this shake recipe ever since. Feel free to use whatever protein powder works for you.

I scoop of your favorite vanilla-flavored protein powder

I tablespoon (15 ml) hemp seeds

I teaspoon (5 ml) goji berry powder

I teaspoon (5 ml) ground cinnamon

½ banana

¼ cup (40 g) frozen broccoli florets

¼ cup (40 g) frozen kale or spinach

3 ice cubes

I cup (240 ml) almond or coconut milk

Shredded coconut for garnish

Blend together in a high-powered blender, and enjoy!

VEGAN EGGNOG

SERVES 1

I was never a huge fan of eggnog, but I always loved the way it looked in *National Lampoon's Christmas Vacation*! Like pumpkin pie, it was something I wanted to like, but just didn't. No matter! I came up with a vegan version that I actually love that also comes close to the taste and texture of the original! Serve it as is, or—if you're feeling naughty—add a kick to it at your holiday party by adding a splash of bourbon or rum. I won't tell.

1 cup (125 g) raw cashews, soaked for at least 4 hours (overnight, preferably)

2 cups (480 ml) filtered water

1 13.5-ounce (380 g) can coconut milk, full-fat

½ cup (120 ml) almond milk

6 large dates, pitted and soaked for an hour

½ medium-size banana

½ teaspoon (5 ml) ground cinnamon

Pinch of nutmeg

Pinch of ground cloves

Pinch of sea salt

1. Blend the drained cashews on high speed with 2 cups (480 ml) of water for at least 2 minutes or until you have a smooth cashew milk.

2. Add the rest of the ingredients and blend again on high speed for about 2 minutes or until smooth.

3. Serve with a sprinkling of cinnamon or a splash of bourbon or rum, if you dare! Enjoy, and happy holidays to you and yours!

Note: This recipe calls for soaked cashews. For best results, soak them overnight. And if not overnight, be sure to soak them at least 4 hours.

Note: This recipe also calls for soaked dates. They need to be soaked for 1 hour.

TURMERIC GINGER TEA

My husband came home from Spain one Christmas with the worst flu he'd ever had. I really didn't want to get it, but the night after he got home, I started getting the telltale signs of a flu coming on: low energy, sore throat, congestion, the whole bit. My friend Melissa Costello of Karma Chow told me about this recipe that she swore by for colds and flus, so I made a beeline for the store and got all the ingredients. I drank a few cups that night and made my husband do the same. In the morning, I felt 100%—no sign of the flu. And my husband—who swore he had the plague—said he felt 100 times better (though he was still sick). Ever since that miracle (it really was a miracle), I have made this tea anytime I'm around someone who is sick, or if I'm starting to feel sick myself. I posted this recipe on my YouTube channel and it has over 173,000 views! So, we must be doing something right.

6 inches (15 cm) of fresh ginger root, peeled and thinly sliced

6 inches (15 cm) of fresh turmeric root, peeled and thinly sliced (or 2 teaspoons of turmeric powder)

8 cups (2 liters) filtered water

Juice of ½ lemon

Optional: 1 teaspoon (5 ml) raw honey or maple syrup

1. Bring the water to a boil in a pot, and then place the ginger and turmeric in the pot. Turn the heat down, and let it simmer for 20 minutes.

2. Place a colander in a large bowl, and strain the ginger and turmeric from the tea water while pouring it from the pot. Add the lemon juice and honey, stir, and enjoy!

3. You can drink this tea hot, or you can store it in the fridge and drink it cold. I like to make a big batch of it and keep it on hand during the week when I feel a cold coming on.

GINGER MINT ICED TEA

SERVES 6 TO 10

I used to make a lot of homemade lemonade. I used to drink the whole batch shamelessly in a day or two. But beside lemons, the other main ingredient was simple syrup (read: white sugar). Thinking about it now, I can't believe that I ever drank the stuff! And I imagine that if I had a sip now, I might pass out on account of the sweetness level. But nothing really compares to a cold glass of lemonade on a hot summer's day, so I had to come up with an alternative that would satisfy me. This recipe for ginger mint iced tea is the perfect alternative. The flavors are delicious enough to stand on their own—they don't need any sweetener to make them shine. Enjoy this on the next hot day when you're craving something refreshing!

1 handful of fresh mint leaves, washed

3 Traditional Medicinals Organic Ginger tea bags

12 cups (3 liters) water, boiled

1. Boil water and place the mint leaves and three ginger tea bags in a glass* or ceramic pitcher. Pour the hot water over the mint leaves and tea bags, and let steep for about 20 to 30 minutes.

2. Remove the tea bags and store the tea in the fridge to cool overnight. Voila—now you have iced tea!

Note: If serving the iced tea within 48 hours, you can leave the mint leaves in the pitcher. If longer than that, take the leaves out or they will start to taste funky! But the tea will keep in the fridge for at least a week.

Safety Tip: Brew the tea and mint leaves in a pot and let cool before pouring into a glass pitcher for storing. Alternatively, run warm water over the pitcher to bring it to room temperature, and place a large metal utensil like a serving spoon into the pitcher, before pouring hot water into it, to conduct the heat and prevent the glass from cracking.

GINGER TULSI TEA

SERVES 6 TO 10

When it's hot outside, I always think back to my childhood iced teas and sodas. When I think about how much sugar I consumed drinking iced tea alone, it makes me shudder! Thankfully, I have lost my taste for too-sweet beverages, but I have certainly not lost my desire for a great iced tea to quench my thirst on a hot summer's day. This recipe not only satisfies that desire, it also packs quite a nutritional punch—without any added sweetness! The ginger aids with digestion, and has a delicious flavor on its own. And the flavors in the tulsi tea add a bit of natural sweetness that make this drink feel like I'm cheating! I tend to have a cup of warm tea, and then put the rest in the fridge to cool. That way, it's always on hand for me to drink whenever I'm feeling thirsty!

12 cups (3 liters) of filtered water

1 handful of fresh ginger, peeled and sliced

1 original tulsi tea bag, original flavor

1. Bring the water to a boil. Once boiling, add in the ginger. Reduce the heat to a simmer, and let the water and ginger simmer together for about 15 to 20 minutes.

2. Strain the ginger out of the water using a colander placed over a large bowl. Toss the ginger away, and steep one bag of tulsi tea in the ginger water for 3 to 5 minutes.

3. Serve hot or cold.

HEMP MILK GINGER TURMERIC CINNAMON LATTE

SERVES 1

This recipe is similar to the almond milk chai latte from earlier on, but rather than using almond milk and chai mix, I use hemp milk, fresh ginger, and a few of the chai spices. Hemp milk is also a little creamier than almond, so it's a bit thicker. I go back and forth between recipes as I see fit. I encourage you to do the same!

3 tablespoons (45 ml or 3-inch long piece/8 cm) fresh ginger, peeled and sliced

1 to 1½ cups (240 to 360 ml) boiled water (depends on the size of your mug)

¾ cup (170 ml) hemp milk (or other preferred milk)

1 teaspoon (5 ml) cinnamon

¼ teaspoon (1 ml) turmeric

1. Place the peeled and sliced ginger in a mug, and pour boiled water into it so that it comes half way up. Set aside to let steep.

2. Steam your hemp milk using either a frother or steamer, or just warm it on the good ol' stove!

3. Pour the hemp milk into the mug with the ginger tea. Stir in the cinnamon and turmeric, and voila—your latte is done!

4. Feel free to sweeten with honey or other sweetener, and enjoy the magic of it all!

SPICED GINGER COCONUT MILK LATTE
SERVES 1

When I was pregnant, I had to stop having my chai tea lattes because of the caffeine. (Yes, I was one of those pregnant rule followers.) But that didn't stop me from craving them (and many other things that were bad for me, whose cravings I did succumb to from time to time). So, I made up my own version of a chai latte using a ginger tea bag instead of a chai bag. The coconut milk changed the taste and made it feel luxurious on account of its thickness, and the spices made me feel like I was indeed drinking a chai latte. Everybody wins!

1 ginger tea bag (I prefer Traditional Medicinals Organic Ginger Aid.)
2 cups (475 ml) water, boiled
¼ cup (60 ml) full fat coconut milk

A pinch each of:
Cinnamon
Cardamom
Nutmeg
Ground cloves
Turmeric
Pepper

1. Get your favorite mug (preferably a large one). Place your tea bag into it. Add a pinch of each of the spices, and then fill the mug with boiled water, leaving enough room to add coconut milk. Steep for one minute.

2. Add coconut milk. Finish off with a sprinkle of your favorite spice. (I like cinnamon.) Drink and enjoy!

mama pose:
breathe,
baby,
breathe

INDEX

Gluten-Free Coconut Banana Chocolate Chip Muffins, 170–171
goat cheese
    Shakshuka, 22–25
    Truffled Mac and (Goat) Cheese, 114–115
goji berries
    Proteins and Greens Shake, 191
    Salted Dark Chocolate Goji Berry Almond Bark, 162–163
Golden Milk, 182, 186
Goldman, Duff, 4
Grainless Granola, 46–47
Grapefruit, Strawberry, Mango Guacamole, 38, 44–45
greens. *See also* salads
    Butternut Squash Alfredo Lasagna with Brazil Nut Parmesan, 86–89
    Collard Green-Wrapped Black Bean Burgers, 100–101
    Ginger Scallion Veggie Bowl, 124–125
    Leeks and Greens Breakfast Bowl, 26–27
    Proteins and Greens Shake, 190–191
    Spirulina Spinach Breakfast Bowl, 34–35
    Sundried Tomato Collard Green Wraps, 116–117
    Warm Spinach Artichoke Dip with Cashew Ricotta Cheese, 40–41
    Weekender Frittata, 18–19
Grilled Veggie Salad with Pesto, 56–57
guacamole, 126–127
    Grapefruit, Strawberry, Mango Guacamole, 44–45

H

hazelnuts
    Arugula and Winter Squash Salad, 74–75
    Chocolate Hazelnut Spread, 138–139
    Grilled Veggie Salad with Pesto, 56–57
    Hazelnut Almond Milk, 188–189
    Raw Banana Blueberry Strawberry Cashew Cheesecake, 156–157
    Summer Salad with Champagne Vinaigrette, 68–69
health coaching, 5
Heirloom Caprese Salad with Grilled Peaches, 76–77
Hemp Milk Ginger Turmeric Cinnamon Latte, 200–201
hemp seeds
    Blueberry Brussels Sprouts Salad with Lemon Vinaigrette, 70–71
    Proteins and Greens Shake, 191
    Your Not-So-Everyday Super Salad, 58–59
honey, salad dressing, 65, 69, 70
hummus, Sweet Pea Hummus, 48–49

I–K

ice cream, Vegan "Cookies and Cream" Milkshake, 164–165
Indian food
    Easy Lentil Dal, 104–105
    Weeknight Veggie Curry, 106–107
Institute for Integrative Nutrition, 5

jicama, Powerhouse Salad, 62–63

kale
    Ginger Scallion Veggie Bowl, 124–125
    Kale Salad with Spicy Almond Dressing, 72–73
    Leeks and Greens Breakfast Bowl, 26–27
    Powerhouse Salad, 62–63
    Spicy Kale and Cauliflower Paleo Rice, 134–135
    Weekender Frittata, 18–19
Kitchari, 128–129
kitchen organization, 7–15
    equipment/tools, 13–15
    freezer, 13
    pantry, 9–12
    refrigerator, 12–13
knives, 13–15

L

lasagna, Butternut Squash Alfredo Lasagna with Brazil Nut Parmesan, 86–89
lattes
    Hemp Milk Ginger Turmeric Cinnamon Latte, 200–201
    Spiced Ginger Coconut Milk Latte, 202–203
    Vanilla Almond Milk Chai Latte, 184–185
Lauren's Veggie Chili, 120–121
leeks
    French Canadian Lentil Soup, 60–61
    Shiitake Leek Sauté, 118–119
Leeks and Greens Breakfast Bowl, 26–27
legumes, 5
    beans. *See* beans
    chickpeas. *See* chickpeas
    lentils. *See* lentils
    peas. *See* peas
lemons/lemon juice
    Beet Sunflower Seed Pesto, 146–147
    lemon vinaigrette, 70–71
    Powerhouse Salad, 62–63
    Spirulina Pesto, 144–145
    Sweet Pea Hummus, 48–49
    Turmeric Ginger Tea, 194–195